THURBER'S DOGS

A Collection of the Master's Dogs,
Written and Drawn, Real and Imaginary,
Living and Long Ago

by

James Thurber

A TOUCHSTONE BOOK
Published by Simon & Schuster, Inc.
NEW YORK

First Touchstone Edition, 1984
Published by Simon & Schuster, Inc.
Simon & Schuster Building
Rockefeller Center
1230 Avenue of the Americas
New York, New York 10020

TOUCHSTONE and colophon are registered trademarks of Simon &
Schuster, Inc.

Manufactured in the United States of America

1 3 5 7 9 10 8 6 4 2 Pbk.

Library of Congress Cataloging in Publication Data

Thurber, James, 1894-1961.
Thurber's dogs.
(A Touchstone book)
1. Dogs—Anecdotes, facetiae, satire, etc. 2. Dogs—
Caricatures and cartoons. I. Title.
PS3539.H94T54   1984   814'.52   84-1279
ISBN 0-671-50598-X Pbk.

FOR SARA THURBER SAUERS

Contents

Foreword, with Figures   xi

The Hound and the Hare   1

1. An Introduction   7
2. How to Name a Dog   15
3. A Preface to Dogs   27
4. The White Rabbit Caper   35
5. Canines in the Cellar   49

Dogs, Women and Men   59

6. A Snapshot of Rex   69
7. The Dog That Bit People   77
8. Josephine Has Her Day   89
9. The Scotty Who Knew Too Much   115
10. The Patient Bloodhound   119

The Hound and the Hat   121

11. Collie in the Driveway   125
12. The Departure of Emma Inch   135
13. The Thin Red Leash   145
14. In Defense of Dogs, Even, After a Fashion, Jeannie   149
15. Look Homeward, Jeannie   159

Contents

16. Blaze in the Sky   169

    A Portfolio   183

17. The Monroes Find a Terminal   197

18. And So to Medve   205

19. Memorial   221

20. Christabel: Part One   225

21. Christabel: Part Two   231

    The Hound and the Gun   243

22. The Cockeyed Spaniard   247

23. Lo, Hear the Gentle Bloodhound!   251

24. A Glimpse of the Flatpaws   279

    The Hound and the Bug   289

Foreword, with Figures

ON THE LAWNS *and porches, and in the living rooms and backyards of my threescore years, there have been more dogs, written and drawn, real and imaginary, than I had guessed, before I started this roundup with the aid of a couple of literary dogcatchers. When we whistled, dogs began appearing from everywhere, including Kansas City. It was as long ago as 1923 that an Ohio newspaper reporter in his twenties, who called himself James Grover Thurber, sold his first short story, "Josephine Has Her Day," to the Kansas City* Star's *Sunday magazine. I have decided that the story has a right to a place in this museum of natural, and personal, history. For a time I considered tinkering with James Grover Thurber's noisy, uninevitable, and improbable climax, which consists of a fight in a grocery store, but I came to the conclusion that this would be wrong, and a kind of tampering with literary evidence. Since I have had thirty-two more writing years than Grover, I would end the story, if I had it to do over, with the wife's buying back Josephine for the fifty dollars she was going to spend on a Scotty. I have apparently always had a suppressed desire to take part in a brawl in a grocery, in partial proof of which I reprint herewith, as Figure I, a drawing from a series called* The War Between Men and Women, *which came out in the 1930's. Grover's only other contribution is "The Thin Red Leash," which appeared in* The New Yorker *in 1926.*

Figure I

Foreword, with Figures

I have done some necessary tinkering throughout this volume, such as replacing time-worn allusions, adding remembered incidents I had left out, and changing titles. Many of the stories and most of the drawings were originally printed in The New Yorker, *but some of them come out of other magazines. I especially want to thank Harper and Brothers for their generous co-operation in making this assembling of canines possible, and Harcourt, Brace, who were also helpful.*

"Collie in the Driveway" appeared in The New Yorker *in 1938 as "Death of a Dog," one of a series of articles under the general title "Where Are They Now?" The accidental killing of Mr. Terhune's collie happened twenty-five years ago, and since I see no reason to perpetuate the ordeal of the Detroit family involved in the accident, I have taken the liberty of giving it a fictional name.*

I have not included dog drawings in which the hound plays only a decorative part. I stuck him into scores of drawings about men and women over the years, when there was white space that needed something to balance the people and the lamps and the chairs. (In those drawings the dog has about the same importance as the pictures on the wall, and doesn't belong in this gallery.) Twenty years ago, my dog was borrowed by D. T. Carlisle for one of the drawings in his "The Belvidere Hounds," and this draw-

Figure II

The Belvidere Hounds unexpectedly checked by the mysterious behavior of a New York guest.

ing is reprinted here, as Figure II, by permission. "The Belvidere Hounds" came out in a special edition of fewer than two thousand copies. I got mine for five dollars, years ago, but the book now costs twenty dollars, and is well worth it.

I have not included, in the prose portion of this book, every piece of mine in which a dog appears, because nobody could lift such a volume, but Feely, for example, is surely as important as Emma Inch in the story about that devoted and inscrutable woman. Some may contend that "The White Rabbit Caper" is a Fred Fox detective story, and that the mastiff and the dachshund merely get in his way. This may be so, but I wanted to put it in, and so I put it in. Another problem arose in the case of "Lavender with a Difference," a section of which is reprinted here as "Canines in the Cellar." I could not very well have left out Judge, the pug dog, and Sampson, the water spaniel, since these were the first dogs the Thurbers ever owned, and the dogs my mother put in the cellar unquestionably deserve a prominent place in this chronicle. I have added a little to this piece, but no butchery of my short biography of my mother has been committed. Anyway, it appears in full in another book. "The Monroes Find a Terminal" was based on an incident involving Medve, and I have added one or two lines to the story, but I have left in, as a kind of relic, a mistake I made which The New

Foreword, with Figures

Yorker's *almost infallible checking department over-looked, the episode of the taxi driving west on Six-teenth Street.*

Seven or eight of the prose items in this museum have never before been published in book form, and a few are entirely new. Publishers like to have such facts mentioned. (Dogs and writers don't much care.) The Introduction, which follows this foreword, is taken from The Fireside Book of Dog Stories *and has been trimmed somewhat to make it fit in here. "A Pre-face to Dogs" was never a preface to any book.*

I had originally intended to reprint a short piece about bloodhounds which I wrote for The New Yorker's *"Talk of the Town" in 1932, but then I met Fancy Bombardier and his owners, Mr. and Mrs. Thomas Sheahan, and their other bloodhounds, and this set me off on a long and fascinating trail. I wish I had had more time on this research, to me the most exciting and rewarding I have engaged in for a long while. Bloodhound-owners are courteous and helpful people, and I mention most of those who so gener-ously assisted my trailing. I want to add, however, the names of Mrs. Robert Noerr of Stamford, Mrs. A. M. Langdale of Sussex, England, and Dr. George Whitney, of New Haven, son of the distinguished Dr. Leon F. Whitney.*

Thurber's Dogs *is dedicated to the first great-grand-child of Mary A. Thurber, who lives at the New Sen-*

eca Hotel in Columbus, Ohio, and is eighty-nine going on ninety as I write this. She still knows and remembers more about Thurber dogs than anyone else in the world.

Christabel, the poodle, is about to become fifteen years old, and since she was given to my daughter when my daughter was nine, and since my daughter now has a daughter of her own, this makes old Christabel, I suppose, what might be called a granddog. She doesn't act like one.

I may have said a few things more than once in this book, and the reader is likely to come upon debatable assertions here and there and small pieces of prejudice or personal bias flapping in the air, but such things are bound to occur in a dog book of any kind, especially one written by a dog man who owned his first dog before the battleship Maine was sunk.

JAMES THURBER

West Cornwall, Connecticut

THURBER'S DOGS

THE HOUND

AND

THE HARE

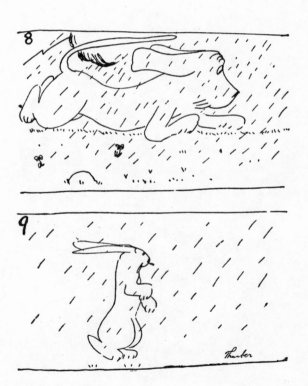

CHAPTER ONE

An Introduction

LEAFING THROUGH Plutarch's *Lives*, on a winter's day, I came upon the story of Xanthippus and his dog. It seems that the old Greek, fleeing Athens one time by ship, left his dog behind—or thought he left him behind. To his amazement and delight, the dog, in the finest whither-thou-goest tradition known to the animal kingdom, plunged into the sea and swam after the galley all the way to Salamis, a feat of which even a seal might well be proud. When the dog died, Xanthippus built a conspicuous tomb for it, high on a windy cliff, that men, infirm of purpose, weak of heart, might be reminded of the miracles which can be wrought by courage, loyalty, and resolution.

Man first gained superiority over the other animals not because of his mind, but because of his fingers.

Thurber's Dogs

He could pick up rocks and throw them, and he could wield a club. Later he developed the spear and the bow and arrow. It is my theory that the other animals, realizing they were as good as cooked if they came within range of Man's weapons, decided to make friends with him. He probably tried to make a pet and companion out of each species in turn. (It never occurred to him, in those days, to play or go hunting with Woman, a peculiarity which has persisted down to the present time.)

It did not take Man long—probably not more than a hundred centuries—to discover that all the animals except the dog were impossible around the house.[1] One has but to spend a few days with an aardvark or a llama, command a water buffalo to sit up and beg, or try to housebreak a moose, to perceive how wisely Man set about his process of elimination and selection. When the first man brought the first dog to his cave (no doubt over and above his wife's protests), there began an association by which Man has enormously profited. It is conceivable that the primordial male held the female, as mate or mother, in no aspect of esteem whatsoever, and that the introduction of the dog into the family circle first infected him with that benign disease known as love. Certain it is that the American male of today, in that remarkable period

---

[1] There is no deliberate intention here to offend admirers of the cat, although I don't really much care whether I do or not.

An Introduction

between infancy and adolescence, goes through a phase, arguably atavistic, during which he views mother, sister, and the little girl next door with cold indifference, if not, indeed, outspoken disdain, the while he lavishes wholehearted affection on Rex or Rover. In his grief over the loss of a dog, a little boy stands for the first time on tiptoe, peering into the rueful morrow of manhood. After this most inconsolable of sorrows, there is nothing life can do to him that he will not be able somehow to bear.

If Man has benefited immeasurably by his association with the dog, what, you may ask, has the dog got out of it? His scroll has, of course, been heavily charged with punishments: he has known the muzzle, the leash, and the tether; he has suffered the indignities of the show bench, the tin can on the tail, the ribbon in the hair; his love life with the other sex of his species has been regulated by the frigid hand of authority, his digestion ruined by the macaroons and marshmallows of doting women. The list of his woes could be continued indefinitely. But he has also had his fun, for he has been privileged to live with and study at close range the only creature with reason, the most unreasonable of creatures.

The dog has got more fun out of Man than Man has got out of the dog, for the clearly demonstrable reason that Man is the more laughable of the two animals. The dog has long been bemused by the singular activities and the curious practices of men, cocking his head inquiringly to one side, intently watching and listening to the strangest goings-on in the world. He has seen men sing together and fight one another in the same evening. He has watched them go to bed when it is time to get up, and get up when it is time to go to bed. He has observed them destroying the soil in vast areas, and nurturing it in small patches. He has stood by while men built strong and solid houses for rest and quiet, and then filled them with lights and bells and machinery. His sensitive nose, which can detect what's cooking in the next township, has caught at one and the same time the bewildering smells of the hospital and the munitions factory. He has seen men raise up great cities to heaven and then blow them to hell.

The effect upon the dog of his life with Man is discernible in his eyes, which frequently are capable of a greater range of expression than Man's. The eyes of the sensitive French poodle, for example, can shine with such an unalloyed glee and darken with so profound a gravity as to disconcert the masters of the earth, who have lost the key to so many of the simpler magics. Man has practiced for such a long time to mask his feelings and to regiment his emotions that some basic quality of naturalness has gone out of both his gaiety and his solemnity.

The dog is aware of this, I think. You can see it in

his eyes sometimes when he lies and looks at you with a long, rueful gaze. He knows that the bare foot of Man has been too long away from the living earth, that he has been too busy with the construction of engines, which are, of all the things on earth, the farthest removed from the shape and intention of nature. I once owned a wise old poodle who used to try to acquaint me with the real facts of living. It was too late, though. I would hastily turn on the radio or run out and take a ride in the car.

The dog has seldom been successful in pulling Man up to its level of sagacity, but Man has frequently dragged the dog down to his. He has instructed it in sloth, pride, and envy; he has made it, in some instances, neurotic; he has even taught it to drink. There once lived in Columbus, Ohio, on Franklin Avenue, a dog named Barge. He was an average kind of dog, medium in size and weight, ordinary in markings. His master and mistress and their two children made up a respectable middle-class family. Some of the young men in the neighborhood, however, pool-shooting, motorcycle-riding bravos, lured Barge into a saloon one day and set before him a saucer of beer. He lapped it up and liked it. From there it was but an easy step to whisky.

Barge was terribly funny, the boys thought, when he got stiff. He would bump into things, hiccup, grin foolishly, and even raise his muzzle on high in what

He goes with his owner into bars.

passed for "Sweet Adeline." Barge's coat became shabby, his gait uncertain, and his eyes misty. He took to staying out in the town all night, raising hell. His duties as watchdog in the home of his owners were completely neglected. One night, when Barge was off on one of his protracted bats, burglars broke in and made off with his mistress' best silver and cut glass.

Barge, staggering home around noon of the next day, sniffed disaster when he was still a block away. His owners were waiting for him grimly on the front porch. They had not straightened up after the burglars. The sideboard drawers were pulled out, the floor littered with napkins and napkin rings. Barge's ears, chops, and tail fell as he was led sternly into the house to behold the result of his wicked way of life. He took one long, sad look around, and the cloudiness cleared from his head. He realized that he was not only a ne'er-do-well but a wrongo. One must guard the house at night, warn the family of fire, pull drowning infants out of the lake. These were the sacred trusts, the inviolable laws. Man had dragged Barge very far down, but there was still a spark of doghood left in him. He ran quickly and quietly upstairs, jumped out of an open window, and killed himself. This is a true and solemn legend of Franklin Avenue.

Dogs suffer from depression.

CHAPTER TWO

How to Name a Dog

EVERY FEW MONTHS somebody writes me and asks if I will give him a name for his dog. Several of these correspondents in the past year have wanted to know if I would mind the use of my own name for their spaniels. Spaniel-owners seem to have the notion that a person could sue for invasion of privacy or defamation of character if his name were applied to a cocker without written permission, and one gentleman even insisted that we conduct our correspondence in the matter through a notary public. I have a way of letting communications of this sort fall behind my roll-top desk, but it has recently occurred to me that this is an act of evasion, if not, indeed, of plain cowardice. I have therefore decided to come straight out with the simple truth that it is as hard for me to think up a name for a dog as it is for anybody else. The idea that I am an expert in the business is probably the outcome of a piece I wrote several years ago, incautiously revealing the fact that I have owned forty or more dogs in my life. This is true, but it is also deceptive. All but five or six of my dogs were disposed of when they were puppies, and I had not gone to the trouble of giving to these impermanent residents of my house any names at all except Shut Up! and Cut That Out! and Let Go!

Names of dogs end up in 176th place in the list of things that amaze and fascinate me. Canine cognomens should be designed to impinge on the ears of dogs and not to amuse neighbors, tradespeople, and casual visitors. I remember a few dogs from the past with a faint but lingering pleasure; a farm hound named Rain, a roving Airedale named Marco Polo, a female bull terrier known as Brody because she liked to jump from moving motor cars and second-story windows, and a Peke called Darien; but that's all.

Well, there is Poker, alias *Fantôme Noir,* a miniature black poodle I have come to know since I wrote the preceding paragraphs. Poker, familiarly known as Pokey, belongs to Mr. and Mrs. J. G. Gude, of White Plains, and when they registered him with the American Kennel Club they decided he needed a

more dignified name. It wasn't easy to explain this
to their youngest child David, and his parents never
did quite clear it up for him. When he was only
eight, David thought the problem over for a long
while and then asked his father solemnly, "If he belongs to that club, why doesn't he ever go there?"
Since I wrote this piece orginally, I have also heard
about a sheep dog named Jupiter, which used to belong to Jimmy Cannon, journalist, critic, and man
about dog shows. He reported in a recent column of
his that Jupiter used to eat geraniums. I have heard
of other dogs that ate flowers, but I refuse to be astonished by this until I learn of one that's downed a
nasturtium.

The only animals whose naming demands concentration, hard work, and ingenuity are the seeing-eye
dogs. They have to be given unusual names because

passers-by like to call to seeing-eyers—"Here, Sport" or "Yuh, Rags" or "Don't take any wooden nickels, Rin Tin Tin." A blind man's dog with an ordinary name would continually be distracted from its work. A tyro at naming these dogs might make the mistake of picking Durocher or Teeftallow. The former is too much like Rover and the latter could easily sound like "Here, fellow" to a dog. Ten years ago I met a young man in his twenties who had been mysteriously blind for nearly five years and had been led about by a seeing-eye German shepherd during all of that time, which included several years of study at Yale. Then suddenly one night the dog's owner began to get his vision back, and within a few weeks was able to read the fine print of a telephone book. The effect on his dog was almost disastrous, and it went into a kind of nervous crack-up, since these animals are trained to the knowledge, or belief, that their owners are permanently blind. After the owner regained his vision he kept his dog, of course, not only because they had become attached to each other but because the average seeing-eye dog cannot be transferred from one person to another.

Speaking of puppies, as I was a while back, I feel that I should warn inexperienced dog-owners who have discovered to their surprise and dismay a dozen puppies in a hall closet or under the floor of the barn, not to give them away. Sell them or keep them, but don't give them away. Sixty per cent of persons who are given a dog for nothing bring him back sooner or later and plump him into the reluctant and unprepared lap of his former owner. The people say that they are going to Florida and can't take the dog, or that he doesn't want to go; or they point out that he eats first editions or lace curtains or spinets, or that he doesn't see eye to eye with them in the matter of housebreaking, or that he makes disparaging remarks under his breath about their friends. Anyway, they bring him back and you are stuck with him—and maybe six others. But if you charge ten or even five dollars for pups, the new owners don't dare return them. They are afraid to ask for their money back because they believe you might think they are hard up and need the five or ten dollars. Furthermore, when a mischievous puppy is returned to its former owner it invariably behaves beautifully, and the person who brought it back is likely to be regarded as an imbecile or a dog-hater or both.

Names of dogs, to get back to our subject, have a range almost as wide as that of the violin. They run from such plain and simple names as Spot, Sport, Rex, Brownie to fancy appellations such as Prince Rudolph Hertenberg Gratzheim of Darndorf-Putzelhorst, and Darling Mist o' Love III of Heather-

Thurber's Dogs

Light-Holyrood—names originated by adults, all of whom in every other way, I am told, have made a normal adjustment to life. In addition to the plain and fancy categories, there are the Cynical and the Coy. Cynical names are given by people who do not like dogs too much. The most popular cynical names during the war were Mussolini, Tojo, and Adolf. I never have been able to get very far in my exploration of the minds of people who call their dogs Mussolini, Tojo, and Adolf, and I suspect the reason is that I am unable to associate with them long enough to examine what goes on in their heads. I nod, and I tell them the time of day, if they ask, and that is all. I never vote for them or ask them to have a drink. The great Coy category is perhaps the largest. The Coy people call their pets Bubbles and Boggles and Sparkles and Twinkles and Doodles and Puffy and Lovums and Sweetums and Itsy-Bitsy and Betsy-Bye-Bye and Sugarkins. I pass these dog-owners at a dog-trot, wearing a horrible fixed grin.

There is a special subdivision of the Coys that is not quite so awful, but awful enough. These people, whom we will call the Wits, own two dogs, which they name Pitter and Patter, Willy and Nilly, Helter and Skelter, Namby and Pamby, Hugger and Mugger, and even Wishy and Washy, Ups and Daisy, Fitz and Startz, Fetch and Carrie, and Pro and Connie.

Thurber's Dogs

Then there is the Cryptic category. These people select names for some private reason or for no reason at all—except perhaps to arouse a visitor's curiosity, so that he will exclaim, "Why in the world do you call your dog *that*?" The Cryptic name their dogs October, Bennett's Aunt, Three Fifteen, Doc Knows, Tuesday, Home Fried, Opus 38, Ask Leslie, and Thanks for the Home Run, Emil. I make it a point simply to pat these unfortunate dogs on the head, ask no question of their owners, and go about my business.

This article has degenerated into a piece that properly should be entitled "How Not to Name a Dog." I was afraid it would. It seems only fair to make up for this by confessing a few of the names I have given my own dogs, with the considerable help, if not, indeed, the insistence, of their mistress. Most of my dogs have been females, and they have answered, with apparent gladness, to such names as Jennie, Tessa, Julie, and Sophie. I have never owned a dog named Pamela, Jennifer, Clarissa, Jacqueline, Guinevere, or Shelmerdene.

About fifteen years ago, when I was looking for a house to buy in Connecticut, I knocked on the front door of an attractive home whose owner, my real-estate agent had told me, wanted to sell it and go back to Iowa to live. The lady agent who escorted me around had informed me that the owner of this place was a man named Strong, but a few minutes after arriving at the house, I was having a drink in the living room with Phil Stong, for it was he. We went out into the yard after a while and I saw Mr. Stong's spaniel. I called to the dog and snapped my fingers, but he seemed curiously embarrassed, like his master. "What's his name?" I asked the latter. He was cornered and there was no way out of it. "Thurber," he said, in a small frightened voice. Thurber and I shook hands, and he didn't seem to me any more depressed than any other spaniel I have met. He had, however, the expression of a bachelor on his way to a party he has tried in vain to get out of, and I think it must have been this cast of countenance that had reminded Mr. Stong of the dog I draw. The dog I draw is, to be sure, much larger than a spaniel and not so shaggy, but I confess, though I am not a spaniel man, that there are certain basic resemblances between my dog and all other dogs with long ears and troubled eyes.

Perhaps I should suggest at least one name for a dog, if only to justify the title of this piece. All right, then, what's the matter with Stong? It's a good name for a dog, short, firm, and effective. I recommend it to all those who have written to me for suggestions and to all those who may be at this very moment turning over in their minds the idea of asking my advice in this difficult and perplexing field of nomenclature.

Thurber's Dogs

Since I first set down these not too invaluable rules for naming dogs, I have heard of at least a dozen basset hounds named Thurber, a Newfoundland called Little Bears Thurber and a bloodhound named Tiffany's Thurber. This is all right with me, so long as the owners of Thurbers do not bring them to call on me at my house in Connecticut without making arrangements in advance. Christabel, my old and imperious poodle, does not like unannounced dog visitors, and tries to get them out of the house as fast as she can. Two years ago a Hartford dog got lost in my neighborhood and finally showed up at my house. He hadn't had much, if anything, to eat for several days, and we fed him twice within three hours, to the high dismay and indignation of Christabel, who only gets one big meal a day. The wanderer was returned to its owner, through a story in the Hartford *Courant,* and quiet descended on my home until a handsome young male collie showed up one night. We had quite a time getting him out of the house. Christabel kept telling him how wonderful it was outdoors and trotting to the door, but the collie wasn't interested. I tried to pick him up, but I am too old to pick up a full-grown collie. In the end Christabel solved the problem herself by leading him outside on the promise of letting him chew one of the bones she had buried. He still keeps coming back to visit us from time to time, but Christabel has hidden her bones in new places. She will romp with the young visitor for about twenty seconds, then show her teeth and send him home. I don't do anything about the situation. After all, my home has been in charge of Christabel for a great many years now, and I never interfere with a woman's ruling a household.

CHAPTER THREE

A Preface to Dogs

As SOON AS A WIFE presents her husband with a child, her capacity for worry becomes acuter: she hears more burglars, she smells more things burning, she begins to wonder, at the theater or the dance, whether her husband left his service revolver in the nursery. This goes on for years and years. As the child grows older, the mother's original major fear—that the child was exchanged for some other infant at the hospital—gives way to even more magnificent doubts and suspicions: she suspects that the child is not bright, she doubts that it will be happy, she is sure that it will become mixed up with the wrong sort of people.

This insistence of parents on dedicating their lives

to their children is carried on year after year in the face of all that dogs have done, and are doing, to prove how much happier the parent-child relationship can become, if managed without sentiment, worry, or dedication. Of course, the theory that dogs have a saner family life than humans is an old one, and it was in order to ascertain whether the notion is pure legend or whether it is based on observable fact that I have for many years made a careful study of the family life of dogs. My conclusions entirely support the theory that dogs have a saner family life than people.

In the first place, the husband leaves on a wood-chuck-hunting expedition just as soon as he can, which is very soon, and never comes back. He doesn't write, makes no provision for the care or maintenance of his family, and is not liable to prosecution because he doesn't. The wife doesn't care where he is, never wonders if he is thinking about her, and although she may start at the slightest footstep, doesn't do so because she is hoping against hope that it is Spot. No lady dog has ever been known to set her friends against her husband or put detectives on his trail.

This same lack of sentimentality is carried out in the mother dog's relationship to her young. For six weeks—but only six weeks—she looks after them religiously, feeds them (they come clothed), washes

their ears, fights off cats, old women, and wasps that
come nosing around, makes the bed, and rescues the
puppies when they crawl under the floor boards of
the barn or get lost in an old boot. She does all these
things, however, without fuss, without that loud and
elaborate show of solicitude and alarm which a
woman displays in rendering some exaggerated service to her child.

At the end of six weeks, the mother dog ceases to lie
awake at night harking for ominous sounds; the next
morning she snarls at the puppies after breakfast, and
routs them all out of the house. "This is forever," she

*At the end of six weeks she tells them to get out and
stay out.*

informs them, succinctly. "I have my own life to live, automobiles to chase, grocery boys' shoes to snap at, rabbits to pursue. I can't be washing and feeding a lot of big six-weeks-old dogs any longer. That phase is definitely over." The family life is thus terminated, and the mother dismisses the children from her mind—frequently as many as eleven at one time—as easily as she did her husband. She is now free to devote herself to her career and to the novel and astonishing things of life.

In the case of one family of dogs that I observed, the mother, a large black dog with long ears and a keen zest for living, tempered only by an immoderate fear of toads and turtles, kicked ten puppies out of the house at the end of six weeks to the day—it was a Monday. Fortunately for my observations, the puppies had no place to go, since they hadn't made any plans, and so they just hung around the barn, now and again trying to patch things up with their mother. She refused, however, to entertain any proposition leading to a resumption of home life, pointing out firmly that she was, by inclination, a chaser of bicycles and a hearth-fire-watcher, both of which activities would be insupportably cluttered up by the presence of ten helpers. The bicycle-chasing field was overcrowded, anyway, she explained, and the hearth-fire-watching field even more so. "We could chase parades together," suggested one of the dogs, but she refused to be touched, snarled, and drove him off.

It is only for a few weeks that the cast-off puppies make overtures to their mother in regard to the re-establishment of a home. At the end of that time, by some natural miracle that I am unable clearly to understand, the puppies suddenly one day don't recognize their mother any more, and she doesn't recognize them. It is as if they had never met, and is a fine idea, giving both parties a clean break and a chance for a fresh start. Once, some months after this particular family had broken up and the pups had been sold, one of them, named Liza, was brought back to "the old nest" for a visit. The mother dog of course didn't recognize the puppy and promptly bit her in the hip. They were separated, each grumbling something about you never know what kind of dogs you're going to meet. Here was no silly affecting reunion, no sentimental tears, no bitter intimations of neglect or forgetfulness or desertion.

If a pup is not sold or given away, but is brought up in the same household with its mother, the two will fight bitterly, sometimes twenty or thirty times a day, for maybe a month. This is very trying to whoever owns the dogs, particularly if they are sentimentalists who grieve because mother and child don't know each other. The condition finally clears up: the two dogs grow to tolerate each other and, beyond growling a little under their breath about how it takes all kinds of dogs to make up a world, get along fairly well together when their paths cross. I know of one mother dog and her half-grown daughter who sometimes spend the whole day together hunting woodchucks, although they don't speak. Their association is not sentimental, but practical, and is based on the fact that it is safer to hunt woodchucks in pairs than alone. These two dogs start out together in the morning, without a word, and come back together in the evening, when they part without saying good night, whether they have had any luck or not. Avoidance of farewells, which are always stuffy and sometimes painful, is another thing in which it seems to me dogs have better sense than people.

Well, one day, the daughter, a dog about ten months old, seemed, by some prank of nature which again I am unable clearly to understand, for a moment or two to recognize her mother after all those months of oblivion. The two had just started out after a fat woodchuck who lived in the orchard. Something felt wrong with the daughter's ear—a long, floppy ear. "Mother," she said, "I wish you'd look at my ear."

Instantly the other dog bristled and growled. "I'm not your mother," she said, "I'm a woodchuck-hunter."

A Preface to Dogs

The daughter grinned. "Well," she said, just to show that there were no hard feelings, "that's not my ear, it's a shortstop's glove."

CHAPTER FOUR

The White Rabbit Caper

(As the Boys Who Turn Out the Mystery Programs
on the Air Might Write a Story for Children)

F RED FOX was pouring himself a slug of rye when
the door of his office opened and in hopped old
Mrs. Rabbit. She was a white rabbit with pink eyes,

and she wore a shawl on her head, and gold-rimmed spectacles.

"I want you to find Daphne," she said tearfully, and she handed Fred Fox a snapshot of a white rabbit with pink eyes that looked to him like a picture of every other white rabbit with pink eyes.

"When did she hop the hutch?" asked Fred Fox.

"Yesterday," said old Mrs. Rabbit. "She is only eighteen months old, and I am afraid that some superstitious creature has killed her for one of her feet."

Fred Fox turned the snapshot over and put it in his pocket. "Has this bunny got a throb?" he asked.

"Yes," said old Mrs. Rabbit. "Franz Frog, repulsive owner of the notorious Lily Pad Night Club."

Fred Fox leaped to his feet. "Come on, Grandma," he said, "and don't step on your ears. We got to move fast."

On the way to the Lily Pad Night Club, old Mrs. Rabbit scampered so fast that Fred Fox had all he could do to keep up with her. "Daphne is my great-great-great-great-great-granddaughter, if my memory serves," said old Mrs. Rabbit. "I have thirty-nine thousand descendants."

"This isn't going to be easy," said Fred Fox. "Maybe you should have gone to a magician with a hat."

"But she is the only one named Daphne," said old

Mrs. Rabbit, "and she lived alone with me on my great carrot farm."

They came to a broad brook. "Skip it!" said Fred Fox.

"Keep a civil tongue in your head, young man," snapped old Mrs. Rabbit.

Just as they got to the Lily Pad, a dandelion clock struck twelve noon. Fred Fox pushed the button on the great green door, on which was painted a white water lily. The door opened an eighth of an inch, and Ben Rat peered out. "Beat it," he said, but Fred Fox shoved the door open, and old Mrs. Rabbit followed him into a cool green hallway, softly but restlessly lighted by thousands of fireflies imprisoned in the hollow crystal pendants of an enormous chandelier. At the right there was a flight of green-carpeted stairs, and at the bottom of the steps the door to the cloakroom. Straight ahead, at the end of the long hallway, was the cool green door to Franz Frog's office.

"Beat it," said Ben Rat again.

"Talk nice," said Fred Fox, "or I'll seal your house up with tin. Where's the Croaker?"

"Once a gumpaw, always a gumpaw," grumbled Ben Rat. "He's in his office."

"With Daphne?"

Thurber's Dogs

"Who's Daphne?" asked Ben Rat.

"My great-great-great-great-great-granddaughter," said old Mrs. Rabbit.

"Nobody's that great," snarled Ben Rat.

Fred Fox opened the cool green door and went into Franz Frog's office, followed by old Mrs. Rabbit and Ben Rat. The owner of the Lily Pad sat behind his desk, wearing a green suit, green shirt, green tie, green socks, and green shoes. He had an emerald tiepin and seven emerald rings. "Whong you wong, Fonnxx?" he rumbled in a cold, green, cavernous voice. His eyes bulged and his throat began to swell ominously.

"He's going to croak," explained Ben Rat.

"Nuts," said Fred Fox. "He'll outlive all of us."

"Glunk," croaked Franz Frog.

Ben Rat glared at Fred Fox. "You oughta go on the stage," he snarled.

"Where's Daphne?" demanded Fred Fox.

"Hoong Dagneng?" asked Franz Frog.

"Your bunny friend," said Fred Fox.

"Nawng," said Franz Frog.

Fred Fox picked up a cello in a corner and put it down. It was too light to contain a rabbit. The front doorbell rang. "I'll get it," said Fred Fox. It was Oliver (Hoot) Owl, a notorious fly-by-night.

The White Rabbit Caper

"What're you doing up at this hour, Hoot?" asked Fred Fox.

"I'm trying to blind myself, so I'll confess," said Hoot Owl testily.

"Confess to what?" snapped Fred Fox.

"What can't you solve?" asked Hoot Owl.

"The disappearance of Daphne," said Fred Fox.

"Who's Daphne?" asked Hoot Owl.

Franz Frog hopped out of his office into the hall. Ben Rat and old Mrs. Rabbit followed him.

Down the steps from the second floor came Sherman Stork, carrying a white muffler or something and grinning foolishly.

"Well, bless my soul!" said Fred Fox. "If it isn't old midhusband himself! What did you do with Daphne?"

"Who's Daphne?" asked Sherman Stork.

"Fox thinks somebody killed Daphne Rabbit," said Ben Rat.

"I *could* be wrong," said Fred Fox, "but I'm not." He pulled open the cloakroom door at the bottom of the steps, and the dead body of a female white rabbit toppled furrily onto the cool green carpet. Her head had been bashed in by a heavy blunt instrument.

"Daphne!" screamed old Mrs. Rabbit, bursting into tears.

"I can't see a thing," said Hoot Owl.

Thurber's Dogs

"It's a dead white rabbit," said Ben Rat. "Anybody can see that. You're dumb."

"I'm wise!" said Hoot Owl indignantly. "I know everything."

"Jeeng Crine," moaned Franz Frog. He stared up at the chandelier, his eyes bulging and his mammoth mouth gaping open. All the fireflies were frightened and went out.

The cool green hallway became pitch dark. There was a shriek in the black, and a feathery "plump." The fireflies lighted up to see what had happened. Hoot Owl lay dead on the cool green carpet, his head bashed in by a heavy blunt instrument. Ben Rat, Franz Frog, Sherman Stork, old Mrs. Rabbit, and Fred Fox stared at Hoot Owl. Over the cool green carpet crawled a warm red stain, whose source was the body of Hoot Owl. He lay like a feather duster.

"Murder!" squealed old Mrs. Rabbit.

"Nobody leaves this hallway!" snapped Fred Fox. "There's a killer loose in this club!"

"I am not used to death," said Sherman Stork.

"Roong!" groaned Franz Frog.

"He says he's ruined," said Ben Rat, but Fred Fox wasn't listening. He was looking for a heavy blunt instrument. There wasn't any.

"Search them!" cried old Mrs. Rabbit. "Somebody has a sap, or a sock full of sand, or something!"

"Yeh," said Fred Fox. "Ben Rat is a sap—maybe someone swung him by his tail."

"You oughta go on the stage," snarled Ben Rat.

Fred Fox searched the suspects, but he found no concealed weapon. "You could have strangled them with that muffler," Fred Fox told Sherman Stork.

"But they were not strangled," said Sherman Stork.

Fred Fox stared at Franz Frog. "You could have scared them to death with your ugly face," he said.

"Bung wung screng ta deng," said Franz Frog.

"You're right," admitted Fred Fox. "They weren't. Where's old Mrs. Rabbit?" he asked suddenly.

"I'm hiding in here," called old Mrs. Rabbit from the cloakroom. "I'm frightened."

Fred Fox got her out of the cool green sanctuary and went in himself. It was dark. He groped around on the cool green carpet. He didn't know what he was looking for, but he found it, a small object lying in a far corner. He put it in his pocket and came out of the cloakroom.

"What'd you find, shamus?" asked Ben Rat apprehensively.

"Exhibit A," said Fred Fox casually.

Thurber's Dogs

"Sahng plang keeng," moaned Franz Frog.

"He says somebody's playing for keeps," said Ben Rat.

"He can say that again," said Fred Fox as the front door was flung open and Inspector Mastiff trotted in, followed by Sergeant Dachshund.

"Well, well, look who's muzzling in," said Fred Fox.

"What have we got here?" barked Inspector Mastiff.

"I hate a private nose," said Sergeant Dachshund.

Fred Fox grinned at him. "What happened to your legs from the knees down, sport?" he asked.

"Drop dead," snarled Inspector Mastiff. "I know Ollie Owl, but who's the twenty-dollar Easter present from Schrafft's?" He turned on Fred Fox. "If this bunny's head comes off and she's filled with candy, I'll have your badge, Fox," he growled.

"She's real, Inspector," said Fred Fox. "Real dead, too. How did you pick up the scent?"

Inspector Mastiff howled. "The Sergeant thought he smelled a rat at the Lily Club," he said. "Wrong again, as usual. Who's this dead rabbit?"

"She's my great-great-great-great-great-grand-daughter," sobbed old Mrs. Rabbit.

Fred Fox lighted a cigarette. "Oh, no, she isn't, sweetheart," he said coolly. "You are *her* great-great-great-great-great-granddaughter." Pink lightning flared in the live white rabbit's eyes. "You killed the old lady, so you could take over her carrot farm," continued Fred Fox, "and then you killed Hoot Owl."

"I'll kill you, too, shamus!" shrieked Daphne Rabbit.

"Put the cuffs on her, Sergeant," barked Inspector Mastiff. Sergeant Dachshund put a pair of handcuffs on the front legs of the dead rabbit. "Not *her,* you dumb kraut!" yelped Inspector Mastiff. It was too late. Daphne Rabbit had jumped through a windowpane and run away, with the Sergeant in hot pursuit.

"All white rabbits look alike to me," growled Inspector Mastiff. "How could you tell them apart—from their ears?"

"No," said Fred Fox. "From their years. The white rabbit that called on me darn near beat me to the Lily Pad, and no old woman can do that."

"Don't brag," said Inspector Mastiff. "Spryness isn't enough. What else?"

"She understood expressions an old rabbit doesn't know," said Fred Fox, "like 'hop the hutch' and 'throb' and 'skip it' and 'sap.' "

"You can't hang a rabbit for her vocabulary," said Inspector Mastiff. "Come again."

Fred Fox pulled the snapshot out of his pocket. "The white rabbit who called on me told me Daphne was eighteen months old," he said, "but read what it says on the back of this picture."

Inspector Mastiff took the snapshot, turned it over, and read, " 'Daphne on her second birthday.' "

"Yes," said Fred Fox. "Daphne knocked six months off her age. You see, Inspector, she couldn't read the writing on the snapshot, because those weren't her spectacles she was wearing."

"Now wait a minute," growled Inspector Mastiff. "Why did she kill Hoot Owl?"

"Elementary, my dear Mastiff," said Fred Fox. "Hoot Owl lived in an oak tree, and she was afraid he saw her burrowing into the club last night, dragging Grandma. She heard Hoot Owl say, 'I'm wise. I know everything,' and so she killed him."

"What with?" demanded the Inspector.

"Her right hind foot," said Fred Fox. "I was looking for a concealed weapon, and all the time she was carrying her heavy blunt instrument openly."

"Well, what do you know!" exclaimed Inspector Mastiff. "Do you think Hoot Owl really saw her?"

"Could be," said Fred Fox. "I happen to think he was bragging about his wisdom in general and not about a particular piece of information, but your guess is as good as mine."

"What did you pick up in the cloakroom?" squeaked Ben Rat.

"The final strand in the rope that will hang

The White Rabbit Caper

Daphne," said Fred Fox. "I knew she didn't go in there to hide. She went in there to look for something she lost last night. If she'd been frightened, she would have hidden when the flies went out, but she went in there after the flies lighted up again."

"That adds up," said Inspector Mastiff grudgingly. "What was it she was looking for?"

"Well," said Fred Fox, "she heard something drop in the dark when she dragged Grandma in there last night and she thought it was a button, or a buckle, or a bead, or a bangle, or a brooch that would incriminate her. That's why she rang me in on the case. She couldn't come here alone to look for it."

"Well, what was it, Fox?" snapped Inspector Mastiff.

"A carrot," said Fred Fox, and he took it out of his pocket, "probably fell out of old Mrs. Rabbit's reticule, if you like irony."

"One more question," said Inspector Mastiff. "Why plant the body in the Lily Pad?"

"Easy," said Fred Fox. "She wanted to throw suspicion on the Croaker, a well-known lady-killer."

"Nawng," rumbled Franz Frog.

"Well, there it is, Inspector," said Fred Fox, "all wrapped up for you and tied with ribbons."

Ben Rat disappeared into a wall. Franz Frog hopped back to his office.

"Mercy!" cried Sherman Stork. "I'm late for an

45

appointment!" He flew to the front door and opened it.

There stood Daphne Rabbit, holding the unconscious form of Sergeant Dachshund. "I give up," she said. "I surrender."

"Is he dead?" asked Inspector Mastiff hopefully.

"No," said Daphne Rabbit. "He fainted."

"I never have any luck," growled Inspector Mastiff.

Fred Fox leaned over and pointed to Daphne's right hind foot. "Owl feathers," he said. "She's all yours, Inspector."

"Thanks, Fox," said Inspector Mastiff. "I'll throw something your way some day."

"Make it a nice, plump Plymouth Rock pullet," said Fred Fox, and he sauntered out of the Lily Pad.

Back in his office, Fred Fox dictated his report on the White Rabbit Caper to his secretary, Lura Fox. "Period. End of report," he said finally, toying with the emerald stickpin he had taken from Franz Frog's green necktie when the fireflies went out.

"Is she pretty?" asked Lura Fox.

"Daphne? Quite a dish," said Fred Fox, "but I like my rabbits stewed, and I'm afraid little Daphne is going to fry."

"But she's so young, Fred!" cried Lura Fox. "Only eighteen months!"

"You weren't listening," said Fred Fox.

"How did you know she wasn't interested in Franz Frog?" asked Lura Fox.

"Simple," said Fred Fox. "Wrong species."

"What became of the candy, Fred?" asked Lura Fox.

Fred Fox stared at her. "What candy?" he asked blankly.

Lura Fox suddenly burst into tears. "She was so soft, and warm, and cuddly, Fred," she wailed.

Fred Fox filled a glass with rye, drank it slowly, set down the glass, and sighed grimly. "Sour racket," he said.

CHAPTER FIVE

Canines in the Cellar

BELINDA WOOLF telephoned my mother at the
Southern Hotel in Columbus one morning a
few years ago and apologized, in a faintly familiar
voice, for never having run in to call on her. Something always seemed to turn up, she declared, to keep
her from dropping by for a visit, and she was sorry.
"I've thought of you, Mrs. Thurber," said Belinda,
"I've thought of you every day since I worked for
you on Champion Avenue. It's been a long time,
hasn't it?" It certainly had. Belinda Woolf was only
twenty-three years old when she came to work for us
as cook in the spring of 1899, and she was seventy-
three when she finally got around to calling her former employer. Exactly half a century had gone by
since my mother had heard her voice. Belinda had
thought of telephoning for more than eighteen thou-

49

sand days, but, as she indicated, more than eighteen thousand things had turned up to prevent her.

About a year after Belinda's appearance out of the past, I went to Columbus, and my mother and I drove out to see her. She is now the wife of Joe Barlow, master carpenter of the Neil House, where Charles Dickens used to stay during his western trips a hundred years ago. In fifty years Belinda had not wandered very far. She was living only two blocks from our old house on South Champion Avenue. The weather was warm, and we sat on the veranda and talked about a night in 1899 that we all remembered. It was past midnight, according to an old clock in the attic of my memory, when Belinda suddenly flung open a window of her bedroom and fired two shots from a .32-caliber revolver at the shadowy figure of a man skulking about in our backyard. Belinda's shooting frightened off the prowler and aroused the family. I was five years old, going on six, at the time, and I had thought that only soldiers and policemen were allowed to have guns. From then on I stood in awe, but not in fear, of the lady who kept a revolver under her pillow. "It was a lonesome place, wasn't it?" said Belinda, with a sigh. "Way out there at the end of nowhere." We sat for a while without talking, thinking about the lonesome place at the end of nowhere.

Number 921 South Champion Avenue is just another house now, in a long row of houses, but when we lived there, in 1899 and 1900, it was the last house on the street. Just south of us the avenue dwindled to a wood road that led into a thick grove of oak and walnut trees, long since destroyed by the southward march of asphalt. Our nearest neighbor on the north was fifty yards away, and across from us was a country meadow that ticked with crickets in the summertime and turned yellow with goldenrod in the fall. Living on the edge of town, we rarely heard footsteps at night, or carriage wheels, but the darkness, in every season, was deepened by the lonely sound of locomotive whistles. I no longer wonder, as I did when I was six, that Aunt Mary Van York, arriving at dusk for her first visit to us, looked about her disconsolately, and said to my mother, "Why in the world do you want to live in this Godforsaken place, Mary?"

Almost all my memories of the Champion Avenue house have as their focal point the lively figure of my mother. I remember her tugging and hauling at a burning mattress and finally managing to shove it out a bedroom window onto the roof of the front porch, where it smoldered until my father came home from work and doused it with water. When he asked his wife how the mattress happened to catch fire, she told him the peculiar truth (all truths in that house were peculiar) that his youngest son, Robert, had set it on fire with a buggy whip. It seemed he had lighted the lash of the whip in the gas grate of the nursery and applied it to the mattress. I also have a vivid memory of the night my mother was alone in the house with her three small sons and set the oil-splashed bowl of a kerosene lamp on fire, trying to light the wick, and herded all of us out of the house, announcing that it was going to explode. We children waited across the street in high anticipation, but the spilled oil burned itself out and, to our bitter disappointment, the house did not go up like a skyrocket to scatter colored balloons among the stars. My mother claims that my brother William, who was seven at the time, kept crying, "Try it again, Mama, try it again," but she is a famous hand at ornamenting a tale, and there is no way of telling whether he did or not.

My brightest remembrance of the old house goes back to the confused and noisy second and last visit of Aunt Mary, who had cut her first visit short because she hated our two dogs—Judge, an irritable old pug, and Sampson, a restless water spaniel—and they hated her. She had snarled at them and they had growled at her all during her stay with us, and not even my mother remembers how she persuaded the old lady to come back for a weekend, but she did, and what is more, she cajoled Aunt Mary into feeding "those dreadful brutes" the evening she arrived.

In preparation for this seemingly simple act of household routine, my mother had spent the afternoon gathering up all the dogs of the neighborhood, in advance of Aunt Mary's appearance, and putting them in the cellar. I had been allowed to go with her on her wonderful forays, and I thought that we were going to keep all the sixteen dogs we rounded up. Such an adventure does not have to have logical point or purpose in the mind of a six-year-old, and I accepted as a remarkable but natural phenomenon my mother's sudden assumption of the stature of Santa Claus.

She did not always let my father in on her elaborate pranks, but he came home that evening to a house heavy with tension and suspense, and she whispered to him the peculiar truth that there were a dozen and a half dogs in the cellar, counting our Judge and Sampson. "What are you up to now, Mame?" he asked her, and she said she just wanted to see Aunt Mary's face when the dogs swarmed up into the kitchen. She could not recall where she had picked up all of the dogs, but I remembered, and still do, that we had imprisoned the Johnsons' Irish terrier, the Eiseles' shepherd, and the Mitchells' fox terrier, among others. "Well, let's get it over with, then," my father said nervously. "I want to eat dinner in peace, if that is possible."

The big moment finally arrived. My mother, full of smiles and insincerity, told Aunt Mary that it would relieve her of a tedious chore—and heaven knows, she added, there were a thousand steps to take in that big house—if the old lady would be good enough to set down a plate of dog food in the kitchen at the head of the cellar stairs and call Judge and Sampson to their supper. Aunt Mary growled and grumbled, and consigned all dogs to the fires of hell, but she grudgingly took the plate and carried it to the kitchen, with the Thurber family on her heels. "Heavenly days!" cried Aunt Mary. "Do you make a ceremony out of feeding these brutes?" She put the plate down and reached for the handle of the door.

None of us has ever been able to understand why bedlam hadn't broken loose in the cellar long before this, but it hadn't. The dogs were probably so frightened by their unique predicament that their belligerence had momentarily left them. But when the door opened and they could see the light of freedom and smell the odor of food, they gave tongue like a pack of hunting hounds. Aunt Mary got the door halfway open and the bodies of three of the largest dogs pushed it the rest of the way. There was a snarling, barking, yelping swirl of yellow and white, black and tan, gray and brindle as the dogs tumbled into the kitchen, skidded on the linoleum, sent the food flying from the plate, and backed Aunt Mary into a corner. "Great God Almighty!" she screamed. "It's a dog factory!" She was only five feet tall, but her counterattack was swift and terrible. Grabbing a broom, she opened the back door and the kitchen windows and began to beat and flail at the army of canines, engaged now in half a dozen separate battles over the scattered food. Dogs flew out the back door and leaped through the windows, but some of them ran upstairs, and three or four others hid under sofas and chairs in the parlor. The indignant snarling and cursing of Judge and Sampson rose above even the laughter of my mother and the delighted squeals of her children. Aunt Mary whammed her way from room to room, driving dogs ahead of her. When the last one had departed and the upset house had been put back in order, my father said to his wife, "Well, Mame, I hope you're satisfied." She was.

Aunt Mary, toward the end of her long life, got the curious notion that it was my father and his sons, and not my mother, who had been responsible for the noisy flux of "all those brutes." Years later, when we visited the old lady on one of her birthdays, she went over the story again, as she always did, touching it up with distortions and magnifications of her own. Then she looked at the male Thurbers in slow, rueful turn, sighed deeply, gazed sympathetically at my mother, and said, in her hollowest tone, "Poor Mary!"

My mother's life with animals had been an arduous one since, as a little girl, she had lost a cranky but beloved parrot which had passed some ugly remarks to a big barnyard rooster and got killed for its impudence. She never owned another bird of any kind after that, but as the mother of three sons, and an admirer of dogs in her own right, she was destined to a life partly made up of canine frolic and frenzy. She once told me about a paraphrase of Longfellow that had been spoken to her in a dream: "And the cares that infest the day shall fold their tents like the Airedales and as silently steal away." This must have come to her, of course, during the troublesome period of the Thurbers' life with Muggs, the Airedale that bit people. But Muggs came later, after Rex, and after quite a series of impermanent strays that Mary Thurber's sons lugged home or that naturally found their way to a house containing three boys. One of these was a young German shepherd that we had picked up at a football game and later restored to its lost owners. Another was an amiable nondescript that turned up one day from nowhere, spent the week end, and silently stole away after eating my youngest brother's starfish, a dead, dried starfish which Robert kept on a table with a shark's tooth and a trap-door spider's nest, which were left untouched.

My grandfather's collie used to spend as much time at our house as at his own, until the advent of Rex. Both the collie and Rex were demon retrievers, fond of chasing a baseball thrown down the street. One day the collie got to the ball first, only to have Rex snatch it from his mouth and bring it back to us on the gallop. The two dogs delayed the fight over this incident until that afternoon in the parlor. It was possibly the longest and certainly the noisiest dogfight ever staged in an American parlor, and there were blood and hair and broken Victrola records and torn lace curtains and smashed ash trays all over the place before we got the battlers separated. The collie, as the aggrieved party, had made the opening slash, and Rex liked nothing better than an opening slash. The long battle ended in a draw and in the departure of the collie for good. He never came back to visit us again.

In later years I set down the brief biographies of both Rex and Muggs, and they appear here in that order.

DOGS, WOMEN AND MEN

"You're a dirty, low-down human being!"

"Here's a study for you, Doctor—he faints."

"Other end, Mr. Pemberton."

"Shut up, Prince! What's biting you?"

"Will you be good enough to dance this outside?"

"I'm very sorry, madam, but the one in the middle is stuffed, poor fellow."

"He's in love with a Basset who moved away."

"Are you two looking for trouble, mister?"

"That's right, now try to win him away from me."

"The father belonged to some people

who were driving through in a Packard."

*"I said the hounds of spring are on winter's traces—
but let it pass, let it pass!"*

*"For heaven's sake, why don't you go outdoors and
trace something!"*

"Well, if I called the wrong number, why did you answer the phone?"

"He's finally got me so that I think I see it, too."

"There go the most intelligent of all animals."

CHAPTER SIX

A Snapshot of Rex

I RAN ACROSS a dim photograph of him the other day, going through some old things. He's been dead about forty years. His name was Rex (my two brothers and I named him when we were in our early teens) and he was a bull terrier. "An American bull terrier," we used to say, proudly; none of your English bulls. He had one brindle eye that sometimes made him look like a clown and sometimes reminded you of a politician with derby hat and cigar. The rest of him was white except for a brindle saddle that always seemed to be slipping off and a brindle stocking on a hind leg. Nevertheless, there was a nobility about him. He was big and muscular and beautifully made. He never lost his dignity even when trying to accomplish the extravagant tasks my brothers and I used to set for him. One of these was the bringing of a ten-foot wooden rail into the yard through the back gate. We would throw it out into the alley and tell him to go get it. Rex was as powerful as a wrestler, and there were not many things that he couldn't manage somehow to get hold of with his great jaws and lift or drag to wherever he wanted to put them, or wherever we wanted them put. He would catch the rail at the balance and lift it clear of the ground and trot with great confidence toward the gate. Of course, since the gate was only four feet wide or so, he couldn't bring the rail in broadside. He found that out when he got a few terrific jolts, but he wouldn't give up. He finally figured out how to do it, by dragging the rail, holding onto one end, growling. He got a great, wagging satisfaction out of his work. We used to bet kids who had never seen Rex in action that he could catch a baseball thrown as high as they could throw it. He almost never let us down. Rex could hold a baseball with ease in his mouth, in one cheek, as if it were a chew of tobacco.

He was a tremendous fighter, but he never started fights. I don't believe he liked to get into them, despite the fact that he came from a line of fighters. He never went for another dog's throat but for one of its ears (that teaches a dog a lesson), and he would get his grip, close his eyes, and hold on. He could hold on for hours. His longest fight lasted from dusk until almost pitch-dark, one Sunday. It was fought in East

A Snapshot of Rex

Main Street in Columbus with a large, snarly non-descript that belonged to a big colored man. When Rex finally got his ear grip, the brief whirlwind of snarling turned to screeching. It was frightening to listen to and to watch. The Negro boldly picked the dogs up somehow and began swinging them around his head, and finally let them fly like a hammer in a hammer throw, but although they landed ten feet away with a great plump, Rex still held on.

The two dogs eventually worked their way to the middle of the car tracks, and after a while two or three streetcars were held up by the fight. A motor-man tried to pry Rex's jaws open with a switch rod; somebody lighted a fire and made a torch of a stick and held that to Rex's tail, but he paid no attention. In the end, all the residents and storekeepers in the neighborhood were on hand, shouting this, suggesting that. Rex's joy of battle, when battle was joined, was almost tranquil. He had a kind of pleasant expression during fights, not a vicious one, his eyes closed in what would have seemed to be sleep had it not been for the turmoil of the struggle. The Oak Street Fire Department finally had to be sent for—I don't know why nobody thought of it sooner. Five or six pieces of apparatus arrived, followed by a battalion chief. A hose was attached and a powerful stream of water was turned on the dogs. Rex held on for several moments more while the torrent buffeted him about like a log in a freshet. He was a hundred yards away from where the fight started when he finally let go.

The story of that Homeric fight got all around town, and some of our relatives looked upon the incident as a blot on the family name. They insisted that we get rid of Rex, but we were very happy with him, and nobody could have made us give him up. We would have left town with him first, along any road there was to go. It would have been different, perhaps, if he had ever started fights, or looked for trouble. But he had a gentle disposition. He never bit a person in the ten strenuous years that he lived, nor ever growled at anyone except prowlers. He killed cats, that is true, but quickly and neatly and without especial malice, the way men kill certain animals. It was the only thing he did that we could never cure him of doing. He never killed or even chased a squirrel. I don't know why. He had his own philosophy about such things. He never ran barking after wagons or automobiles. He didn't seem to see the idea in pursuing something you couldn't catch, or something you couldn't do anything with, even if you did catch it. A wagon was one of the things he couldn't tug along with his mighty jaws, and he knew it. Wagons, therefore, were not a part of his world.

Swimming was his favorite recreation. The first time he ever saw a body of water (Alum Creek), he trotted nervously along the steep bank for a while, fell to barking wildly, and finally plunged in from a height of eight feet or more. I shall always remember that shining, virgin dive. Then he swam upstream and back just for the pleasure of it, like a man. It was fun to see him battle upstream against a stiff current, struggling and growling every foot of the way. He had as much fun in the water as any person I have known. You didn't have to throw a stick in the water to get him to go in. Of course, he would bring back a stick to you if you did throw one in. He would even have brought back a piano if you had thrown one in.

That reminds me of the night, way after midnight, when he went a-roving in the light of the moon and brought back a small chest of drawers that he had found somewhere—how far from the house nobody ever knew; since it was Rex, it could easily have been half a mile. There were no drawers in the chest when he got it home, and it wasn't a good one—he hadn't taken it out of anybody's house; it was just an old cheap piece that somebody had abandoned on a trash heap. Still, it was something he wanted, probably because it presented a nice problem in transportation. It tested his mettle. We first knew about his achievement when, deep in the night, we heard him trying to get the chest up onto the porch. It sounded as if two or three people were trying to tear the house down. We came downstairs and turned on the porch light. Rex was on the top step trying to pull the thing up, but it had caught somehow and he was just holding his own. I suppose he would have held his own till dawn if we hadn't helped him. The next day we carted the chest miles away and threw it out. If we had thrown it out in a near-by alley, he would have brought it home again, as a small token of his integrity in such matters. After all, he had been taught to carry heavy wooden objects about, and he was proud of his prowess.

I am glad Rex never saw a trained police dog jump. He was just an amateur jumper himself, but the most daring and tenacious I have ever seen. He would take on any fence we pointed out to him. Six feet was easy for him, and he could do eight by making a tremendous leap and hauling himself over finally by his paws, grunting and straining; but he lived and died without knowing that twelve- and sixteen-foot walls were too much for him. Frequently, after letting him try to go over one for a while, we would have to carry him home. He would never have given up trying.

There was in his world no such thing as the impossible. Even death couldn't beat him down. He died, it is true, but only as one of his admirers said, after "straight-arming the death angel" for more than an hour. Late one afternoon he wandered home, too slowly and too uncertainly to be the Rex that had trotted briskly homeward up our avenue for ten years. I think we all knew when he came through the gate that he was dying. He had apparently taken a terrible beating, probably from the owner of some dog that he had got into a fight with. His head and body were scarred. His heavy collar with the teeth marks of many a battle on it was awry; some of the big brass studs in it were sprung loose from the leather. He licked at our hands and, staggering, fell, but got up again. We could see that he was looking for someone. One of his three masters was not home. He did not get home for an hour. During that hour the bull terrier fought against death as he had fought against the cold, strong current of Alum Creek, as he had fought to climb twelve-foot walls. When the person he was waiting for did come through the gate, whistling, ceasing to whistle, Rex walked a few wabbly paces toward him, touched his hand with his muzzle, and fell down again. This time he didn't get up.

CHAPTER SEVEN

The Dog That Bit People

PROBABLY NO ONE MAN should have as many dogs in his life as I have had, but there was more pleasure than distress in them for me except in the case of an Airedale named Muggs. He gave me more trouble than all the other fifty-four or -five put together, although my moment of keenest embarrassment was the time a Scotch terrier named Jeannie, who had just had four puppies in the shoe closet of a fourth-floor apartment in New York, had the fifth and last at the corner of—but we shall get around to that later on. Then, too, there was the prize-winning French poodle, a great big black poodle—none of your little, untroublesome white miniatures—who got sick riding in the rumble seat of a car with me on her way to the Greenwich Dog Show. She had a red rubber bib tucked around her throat and, since a rainstorm came up when we were halfway through the Bronx, I had to hold over her a small green umbrella, really more of a parasol. The rain beat down fearfully, and suddenly the driver of the car drove into a big garage, filled with mechanics. It happened so quickly that I forgot to put the umbrella down, and I shall always remember the look of incredulity that came over the face of the garageman who came over to see what we wanted. "Get a load of this, Mac," he called to someone behind him.

But the Airedale, as I have said, was the worst of all my dogs. He really wasn't my dog, as a matter of fact; I came home from a vacation one summer to find that my brother Robert had bought him while I was away. A big, burly, choleric dog, he always acted as if he thought I wasn't one of the family. There was a slight advantage in being one of the family, for he didn't bite the family as often as he bit strangers. Still, in the years that we had him he bit everybody but Mother, and he made a pass at her once but missed. That was during the month when we suddenly had mice, and Muggs refused to do anything about them. Nobody ever had mice exactly like the mice we had that month. They acted like pet mice, almost like mice

The Dog That Bit People

somebody had trained. They were so friendly that one night when Mother entertained at dinner the Friraliras, a club she and my father had belonged to for twenty years, she put down a lot of little dishes with food in them on the pantry floor so that the mice would be satisfied with that and wouldn't come into the dining room. Muggs stayed out in the pantry with the mice, lying on the floor, growling to himself—not at the mice, but about all the people in the next room that he would have liked to get at. Mother slipped out into the pantry once to see how everything was going. Everything was going fine. It made her so mad to see Muggs lying there, oblivious of the mice—they came running up to her—that she slapped him and he slashed at her, but didn't make it. He was sorry immediately, Mother said. He was always sorry, she said, after he bit someone, but we could not understand how she figured this out. He didn't act sorry.

Mother used to send a box of candy every Christmas to the people the Airedale bit. The list finally contained forty or more names. Nobody could understand why we didn't get rid of the dog. I didn't understand it very well myself, but we didn't get rid of him. I think that one or two people tried to poison Muggs—he acted poisoned once in a while—and old Major Moberly fired at him once with his service revolver near the Seneca Hotel in East Broad Street—

Thurber's Dogs

but Muggs lived to be almost eleven years old, and even when he could hardly get around, he bit a congressman who had called to see my father on business. My mother had never liked the congressman—she said the signs of his horoscope showed he couldn't be trusted (he was Saturn with the moon in Virgo)— but she sent him a box of candy that Christmas. He sent it right back, probably because he suspected it was trick candy. Mother persuaded herself it was all for the best that the dog had bitten him, even though father lost an important business association because of it. "I wouldn't be associated with such a man," Mother said. "Muggs could read him like a book."

We used to take turns feeding Muggs to be on his good side, but that didn't always work. He was never in a very good humor, even after a meal. Nobody knew exactly what was the matter with him, but whatever it was it made him irascible, especially in the mornings. Robert never felt very well in the morning, either, especially before breakfast, and once when he came downstairs and found that Muggs had moodily chewed up the morning paper he hit him in the face with a grapefruit and then jumped up on the dining-room table, scattering dishes and silverware and spilling the coffee. Muggs' first free leap carried him all the way across the table and into a brass fire screen in front of the gas grate, but he was back on his feet in a moment, and in the end he got Robert and gave him a pretty vicious bite in the leg. Then he was all over it; he never bit anyone more than once at a time. Mother always mentioned that as an argument in his favor; she said he had a quick temper but that he didn't hold a grudge. She was forever defending him. I think she liked him because he wasn't well. "He's not strong," she would say, pityingly, but that was inaccurate; he may not have been well but he was terribly strong.

One time my mother went to the Chittenden Hotel to call on a woman mental healer who was lecturing in Columbus on the subject of "Harmonious Vibrations." She wanted to find out if it was possible to get harmonious vibrations into a dog. "He's a large tan-colored Airedale," Mother explained. The woman said she had never treated a dog, but she advised my mother to hold the thought that he did not bite and would not bite. Mother was holding the thought the very next morning when Muggs got the iceman, but she blamed that slip-up on the iceman. "If you didn't think he would bite you, he wouldn't," Mother told him. He stomped out of the house in a terrible jangle of vibrations.

One morning when Muggs bit me slightly, more or less in passing, I reached down and grabbed his short stumpy tail and hoisted him into the air. It was a fool-hardy thing to do and the last time I saw my mother, about six months ago, she said she didn't know what possessed me. I don't either, except that I was pretty mad. As long as I held the dog off the floor by his tail he couldn't get at me, but he twisted and jerked so, snarling all the time, that I realized I couldn't hold him that way very long. I carried him to the kitchen and flung him onto the floor and shut the door on him just as he crashed against it. But I forgot about the back stairs. Muggs went up the back stairs and down the front stairs and had me cornered in the living room. I managed to get up onto the mantelpiece above the fireplace, but it gave way and came down with a tremendous crash, throwing a large marble clock, several vases, and myself heavily to the floor. Muggs was so alarmed by the racket that when I picked myself up he had disappeared. We couldn't find him anywhere, although we whistled and shouted, until old Mrs. Detweiler called after dinner that night. Muggs had bitten her once, in the leg, and she came into the living room only after we assured her that Muggs had run away. She had just seated herself when, with a great growling and scratching of claws, Muggs emerged from under a davenport where he had been quietly hiding all the time, and bit her again. Mother examined the bite and put arnica on it and told Mrs. Detweiler that it was only a bruise. "He just bumped you," she said. But Mrs. Detweiler left the house in a nasty state of mind.

Lots of people reported our Airedale to the police, but my father held a municipal office at the time and was on friendly terms with the police. Even so, the cops had been out a couple of times—once when Muggs bit Mrs. Rufus Sturtevant and again when he bit Lieutenant-Governor Malloy—but Mother told them that it hadn't been Muggs' fault but the fault of the people who were bitten. "When he starts for them, they scream," she explained, "and that excites him." The cops suggested that it might be a good idea to tie the dog up, but Mother said that it mortified him to be tied up and that he wouldn't eat when he was tied up.

Muggs at his meals was an unusual sight. Because of the fact that if you reached toward the floor he would bite you, we usually put his food plate on top of an old kitchen table with a bench alongside the table. Muggs would stand on the bench and eat. I remember that my mother's Uncle Horatio, who boasted that he was the third man up Missionary Ridge, was splutteringly indignant when he found out that we fed the dog on a table because we were afraid to put his plate on the floor. He said he wasn't afraid of any dog that ever lived and that he would put the dog's plate on the floor if we would give it to him. Robert said that if Uncle Horatio had fed Muggs on the ground just before the battle he would have been the first man up Missionary Ridge. Uncle Horatio was furious. "Bring him in! Bring him in now!" he shouted. "I'll feed the ———— on the floor!" Robert was all for giving him a chance, but my father wouldn't hear of it. He said that Muggs had already been fed. "I'll feed him again!" bawled Uncle Horatio. We had quite a time quieting him.

In his last year Muggs used to spend practically all of his time outdoors. He didn't like to stay in the house for some reason or other—perhaps it held too many unpleasant memories for him. Anyway, it was hard to get him to come in, and as a result the garbage man, the iceman, and the laundryman wouldn't come near the house. We had to haul the garbage down to the corner, take the laundry out and bring it back, and meet the iceman a block from home. After this had gone on for some time, we hit on an ingenious arrangement for getting the dog in the house so that we could lock him up while the gas meter was read, and so on. Muggs was afraid of only one thing, an electrical storm. Thunder and lightning frightened him out of his senses (I think he thought a storm had broken the day the mantelpiece fell). He would rush into the house and hide under a bed or in a clothes closet. So

Thunderstorms have driven more than one dog into hysterics.

we fixed up a thunder machine out of a long narrow piece of sheet iron with a wooden handle on one end. Mother would shake this vigorously when she wanted to get Muggs into the house. It made an excellent imitation of thunder, but I suppose it was the most roundabout system for running a household that was ever devised. It took a lot out of Mother.

A few months before Muggs died, he got to "seeing things." He would rise slowly from the floor, growling low, and stalk stiff-legged and menacing toward nothing at all. Sometimes the Thing would be just a little to the right or left of a visitor. Once a Fuller Brush salesman got hysterics. Muggs came wandering into the room like Hamlet following his father's ghost. His eyes were fixed on a spot just to the left of the Fuller Brush man, who stood it until Muggs was about three slow, creeping paces from him. Then he shouted. Muggs wavered on past him into the hallway, grumbling to himself, but the Fuller Brush man went on shouting. I think Mother had to throw a pan of cold water on him before he stopped. That was the way she used to stop us boys when we got into fights.

Muggs died quite suddenly one night. Mother wanted to bury him in the family plot under a marble stone with some such inscription as "Flights of angels sing thee to thy rest" but we persuaded her it was against the law. In the end we just put up a smooth board above his grave along a lonely road. On the board I wrote with an indelible pencil *"Cave Canem."* Mother was quite pleased with the simple, classic dignity of the old Latin epitaph.

CHAPTER EIGHT

Josephine Has Her Day

THE DICKINSONS' PUP was a failure. A bull terrier, a female, and a failure. With all of life before her, she had suddenly gone into a decline.

"She is pining away," said Dick, "like a mid-Victorian lady whose cavalier rode off and never came back."

"No," said Ellen, "there's nothing romantic about her. She looks like a servant girl who has been caught stealing a bar pin."

The failure, which was spiritual as well as physical, was unaccountable. Three weeks before, the pup had been bright and waggly and rotund. Ellen, discovering it in a bird store yapping at the virulent green tail of an indignant lady parrot, had called it not only a little plum-plum, but also a little umpsy-dumpsy.

Thus one thing had led to another, including momentary forgetfulness of their original intention to buy a Scotch terrier, mitigation of the crime being a female and a bull terrier, and eventual purchase of the puppy. And now here she had been shipped to their summer cottage in the Adirondacks, covered with gloom and sulphur, the shadow of her former self. They sat above her, the first hour of her arrival, in grim judgment.

"Maybe she's just growing," said Dick hopefully.

"An idiot could see she's shrinking," said Ellen. "Of course, you would have a bull terrier."

"I don't think it is a bull terrier, now," said Dick.

"Well, it *was* a bull terrier. And a female, too! What ever possessed us!"

"You called her a little plum-plum," murmured Dick.

"And you bought her," retorted Ellen. "Well, she'll have to be fed, I suppose. There wasn't a thing to eat in that shipping box." She swooped up the little dog. Now that it was so thin and its excess skin so wrinkly, a curious black edging around its eyes and jaw completed an effect of the most profound melancholy.

The puppy gave only two depressed laps at the milk-soaked bread placed before her, and then wobbled over to the stove in the sitting room, revolved uncertainly three times, and closed her eyes with a pessimistic sigh.

Josephine Has Her Day

"Well, sir, she's a nice doggy," said Dick generously, starting over to her, "yes, sir, she's a nice doggy." But his wife intervened.

"Mustn't do that," she warned. "It says in the puppy book not to disturb them at their normal sleeping hours." Mrs. Dickinson had bought a lovely puppy book, illustrated with pictures of bright and waggly puppies.

When they went to bed the puppy was sleeping soundly on a bed they fixed for it in a corner of the kitchen, apparently glad to rest after the long, jolting ride. This gladness, however, did not carry her through the night. When the stars were still bright the Dickinsons were aroused from sleep by a clamorous yelping, a wonderfully able and lusty yelping for such a despondent puppy.

"Good Lord!" groaned Dickinson. "Now what?"

"They are bound to yelp the first few nights," said his wife, sleepily.

"Doesn't it say anything in the book about their not disturbing us at our normal sleeping hours?" demanded Dickinson. "Can't I go out and shut her up, do you suppose?"

"No. It would encourage her to expect a response every time she howled, and if you humor them that way they would soon get the upper hand."

"Well, if she keeps this up she'll get it anyway," grumbled Dick as he stuffed the ends of his pillow into his ears. "The National Association of Puppies probably hired the man to write that book."

The next morning at his typewriter Dickinson felt his mind being drawn, slowly but relentlessly, away from the necessary concentration on his work. Something was striking into his brain like the measured thud of a distant drum. "Come ... come ... come."

It was his wife's voice emerging from the "secluded room." Gradually a note of exasperation crept in. It was followed by the sound of a slight scratching body being dragged across the floor. There were more "comes," a silence, and more scratching. Then very insistent "comes," but no scratching.

"Is she dead, dear?" called out Dick hopefully.

His wife came into the room, carrying the pessimistic-looking puppy, still saffron with the sulphur that, Dick hazarded, had been showered upon her in the interest of "bug prevention."

"She seems listless," said Mrs. Dickinson. "Do you suppose she was the runt of a litter? The book says to avoid the runts."

"Napoleon was a runt," observed Dick sagely.

"But not of a litter," responded his wife.

"By golly," exclaimed Dick suddenly. "I've got a name for her, anyway! We'll call her Josephine!"

"Josephine?"

"Yes. After the wife of Napoleon, the famous runt. She started well, but got sort of 'down and out.' "

Josephine Has Her Day

Mrs. Dickinson dropped wearily into a chair and put the puppy on the floor. "Well, I've tried to make this thing come to me all morning, and she just sits and studies the floor with that darned frown."

"Maybe she just doesn't want to come," said Dick.

"That's no reason why she shouldn't. The book says it is almost certain—wait a minute, I'll read it to you." She opened the puppy book which she carried in one hand. "Here: 'It is almost certain that you will be unexpectedly delighted during the very first lesson by their sudden scampering comprehension and that you will perceive they accept your word as law.' "

They watched the little dog study the carpet with incurious attention.

"Lawless little beast," mused Dick. "Look out if she begins to trace the design of the carpet with her paw. It's a sure sign of the end."

"No such luck," said Ellen with some bitterness.

Dick leaned down nearer the puppy. "Josephine!" he cried loudly but firmly. The puppy looked up at him as a little old lady on a train, constantly afraid of being carried past her station, might look at her carefree traveling companions. "She knows her name, anyway, and if she didn't have this awful thing on her mind she might scamper with comprehension, or whatever it is they do."

"Oh, I don't think she has any mind," cried Mrs. Dickinson, irritably. "But there—the book says that

93

calmness, toleration, and self-control are essential in training a puppy."

"That book certainly says a lot for such a little book," commented Dick.

"And for such a little puppy," said his wife scornfully, as she picked up Josephine and carried her outdoors.

As the days went on, Josephine seemed to have taken the stigma of runt literally, as a thing to be religiously lived up to. She remained undeveloped physically and, Mrs. Dickinson declared, mentally, too. She declined, with stolid indifference, in her lesson hour, to adhere to any of the rules of the puppy book. The gay enterprise of "fetch" seemed to create in her no emotion save perhaps a vague wonder as to why the bit of rolled-up paper was tossed about so often.

At length came a cold, drizzly Monday when the Dickinsons gave up. They had had the empress more than three weeks, and her favorite occupation was to sit near the stove, frowning dejectedly and quivering. Once she turned over a cold wood ash with her paw. But that was all.

"Let's give her away to some family around here," said Dick, finally. "They all have lots of kids who would be crazy to have her."

"Yes, and they all have lots of dogs," said Ellen,

"big, virile, happy dogs. Besides, no one wants anything but a hound dog, a hunter, in this country."

"I still think we might find some family that would take her. Someone's dog may have died."

"Everybody has two or three dogs. They wouldn't all die."

"They might," said Dick, hopefully. "They might have been playing with the shotgun, not knowing it was loaded."

"Nobody would look at a runt, a female whatnot. They would laugh just to see us walking along with her."

"We won't walk—we'll hire the Blanchards' flivver and tour around hunting a home for her," said Dick, enlarging on his plan.

So the next morning, which dawned with a promising sun, they started off with Josephine, the condemned puppy that wouldn't grow and wouldn't learn, shivering and frowning at the wind in dismay. Every house they passed for several miles had a hound dog, or two or three, big-pawed, long-eared creatures, nosing about the grounds. At last, however, when they tried their luck on a dirt byroad, they saw a small brown house hanging on a hillside, from whose environs came no mournful baying.

Dick stopped the car a little way down the road, bundled the puppy in his arms and got out. There he paused. The bright sun had been overcome by one of those rapidly driving caravans of dark clouds that ride the ranges of the north in the springtime. It began to rain. Dick put up his coat collar.

"Why shall I say we don't want her?" he asked his wife.

"Oh, just act bighearted," she laughed cheerily. "They might think you are Santa Claus."

But Dick's confidence in his own scheme melted rapidly in the rain as he carried the distressed and quivering puppy toward the front gate of the silent, weathered house. As he reached the slate-colored mail box, which winds and rain had beaten to a dejected slant, the puppy began to behave in a singular fashion. Her insides, as Dick described it later, began to go up and down. He turned and carried Josephine quickly back to Mrs. Dickinson.

"She's dying," he said, handing her to his wife.

"Hiccups, silly," said Ellen. "She'll get over them. It's nothing."

"No decent family would want a dog with hiccups," said Dick, firmly.

So they decided to wait until the paroxysms were over. This meant an unusually long wait. Josephine proved to be an accomplished hiccuper. If an interval was so protracted as to give hope of cessation, the next hiccup was so violent as to threaten indefinite continuance. At length Dick knocked the ashes from his pipe determinedly, got out of the car and lifted Josephine down after him. He set her in the road. Then suddenly he leaped at her and barked.

The puppy plunged down into the ditch by the roadside, her ears flatly inside out in abject terror. Dick hurried after her and retrieved a very wet and very muddy Josephine.

"Have you lost your mind?" exclaimed his wife. But Dickinson held up Josephine and examined her carefully. There were no more hiccups.

"By golly," he said, "these home remedies are the goods."

He started for the house again, briskly, the dog under his arm. After a long time the door on which he gingerly knocked opened just wide enough to frame the hard, spare face of a woman.

"Well, what do you want?" she growled ominously. Josephine growled ominously, too.

"I—us—" began Dick. "That is . . . er . . . a . . . can you tell me how far it is to Dale?"

Dale was the town on the outskirts of which the Dickinsons lived, the town from which they had just come. The woman jerked her thumb.

"Two mile," she grunted.

Josephine growled. The woman slammed the door. Dick walked back to his wife.

"She said her husband won't have a dog about the place," he told her. "Seems his father was bitten by one and the boys all inherited this dread."

Thurber's Dogs

The kind-faced lady who came to the door of the next place lifted her hands in polite refusal. Land! she already had two dogs! And Rex had a sore on his leg. Did the gentleman know what to do for sores on the leg? Dick said proudly that Josephine never had sores on the leg. "Maybe Eli Madden, the storekeeper in Dale, would take it," added the lady after a moment. "His dog was gored by a bull a week back—well, no—two weeks come Monday. You might try there. Sometimes we think Rex was bit by a woodchuck." Dick said Josephine had never been bitten by a woodchuck, and thanked the lady.

They whirled back over the road to Madden's place, which was not far from their cottage. It happened that school was letting out and the streets were filled with children. They seemed suddenly with economy of movement to surround the Dickinsons as they got out of the car and put Josephine on the ground to stretch. She studied the insurmountable problem of dust with furrowed brow.

"Lookut the lion," yelled one boy. "Woo! woo!"

"What kind of a dog it it, mister?" asked another.

"Aw, that ain't no dog," jeered a third.

"This," said Dick, "is a very wonderful dog. We are walking around the world with it. It eats keys."

"Dick!" said his wife.

"Eats keys?" exclaimed the children in a grand chorus.

Josephine Has Her Day

"Trunk keys, door keys, padlock keys—any kind of keys," said Dick. "It shakes them well before eating."

Mrs. Dickinson indignantly picked up Josephine and led the way into Madden's store. "Heavens!" she said to her husband as the door shut out the parting jeers of the skeptical children, "Don't ever do that again. It's bad enough to have such a dog without summoning spectators."

She walked to the counter as Eli Madden came into the store from a back room. "We understand," she said sweetly, "that you lost your dog recently and would like to have another one."

"Gored by a bull," said Madden.

"We have a splendid puppy here, an American hound terrier," pursued Mrs. Dickinson brightly. Dick coughed loudly and hurriedly.

"That is—a bull terrier, an American bull terrier," he said. "It's yours for the taking."

"I tell you," said Madden, picking up the dog and examining it as if it were a motor car part, "it's too young a dog for me to bother with. But Floyd Timmons might take her. Never seen a stray yit he wouldn't. If you say so I'll take her up when I go this evening. I drive right past Floyd's place."

"If you don't mind," said Mrs. Dickinson eagerly.

Just then Josephine sneezed.

"She ain't sick, is she?" asked Madden suspiciously.

Thurber's Dogs

"She never did that before," exclaimed Mrs. Dickinson.

"May be distemper," said Madden, spitting. Josephine sniffled and looked miserable.

"Well, has she got a cold?" cooed Mrs. Dickinson, picking her up. "Has she got a little cold?"

They arranged with Madden to bring the dog back when it was quite over its cold. But for a week Josephine sneezed and sniffled at frequent intervals and her nose remained very warm. Mrs. Dickinson fixed a warmer bed for her, heated the shawl on which she slept, and placed a blanket under that; she fed her meat broth every day and studied the puppy book carefully for further suggestions. On the eighth day Josephine was over her sniffling and seemed much brighter than she had ever been. She even romped a bit and tugged at an apron string that Mrs. Dickinson playfully shook in front of her. "That's a real bulldog trait," said Dick admiringly.

They took her out into the front yard and the puppy scampered about a little on the grass, and even barked, a plaintive bark, at a vagrant scrap of paper. While they were watching her with amusement a man drove up to the end of the walk in a buggy.

"Have you got a dog here you don't want?" he sang out cheerfully. "My name's Timmons." The Dickinsons rose from where they were sitting on the porch.

Josephine Has Her Day

"Oh, yes," said Dickinson cordially, "yes—sure."

The man got out of his buggy and came toward the house. And immediately Josephine retreated a step toward her master and mistress and growled, a tiny, funny growl.

"Quite a watchdog," said the man. "Here, pup." He stooped down and picked her up. She yielded with a wild look at Mrs. Dickinson. "You still want to part with her?"

"We really want a Scotch terrier," Dick told him. "That's the reason we are giving her up."

"I see," said the man. He shifted the dog to an easier position.

"Be sure she has a warm place to sleep," said Mrs. Dickinson, following Timmons to his buggy. "We aren't letting her sleep outdoors yet. She doesn't stand cold very well. She has had a cold and just got over it. Maybe you would want to take along the bed she has been using?"

"Oh, we got plenty of warm stuff we can bed her down in. We'll keep her in the kitchen of nights until it warms up a bit."

"She shouldn't be fed much cooked meat," went on Mrs. Dickinson. "If you could see that she got some broth now and then and some lean meat, well cut up. Milk isn't so good for her, so we don't give her much of it."

Timmons tucked the dog into the robe by his side.

Josephine peered with questioning eyes first at her new owner and then at her recent mistress.

"Now, I'd be willing to pay you a little something for her. You see, a bull terrier will come in handy with the cows when my other dogs git too old, or die off."

"Not at all," said Dick.

"Oh, no," said Mrs. Dickinson. "Her name is Josephine," she added.

"Oh, that's all right," said Timmons largely. He clucked to his horse and the buggy moved off. They had a glimpse of Josephine peering back from one end of the seat, and then a hand took her out of sight.

"Well, there's a big bother off your hands," said Dick cheerfully, and Mrs. Dickinson nodded assent.

Scarcely an hour of the next few days went by, however, without some remembrance of Josephine coming up between them. There was, for one thing, the puppy book, rather useless now; and the little bed in the corner to stumble over; and the stick with a piece of paper tied on one end that Mrs. Dickinson had made for a plaything; and puppy biscuits scattered about the house and grounds. After a week, however, Dickinson, absorbed in his work, had almost forgotten the dog. Then one noon at luncheon he was outlining to his wife a plot for a story. It was a tale of motored action, set in the mountain ways, with rumrunners and deputy sheriffs and a girl in a red roadster driving madly through it.

"Then," explained Dick, "as they near the old house, which they suppose abandoned, a dog suddenly barks——"

"I do hope he will feed her the right things," said Mrs. Dickinson.

Dick put the brakes to his careening motor cars.

"Who will feed what?"

"Josephine," said his wife.

"Still thinking of the empress, eh?"

"You know a man is so likely to be careless. I wish I could have spoken to his wife about her."

"She'll be all right," said Dick brightly, pushing the dish of strawberry jam nearer to Ellen. "And when we get that Scotty in New York this fall you'll forget all about her and be glad we got her a good home."

"She was mighty bright and fine that last day," mused his wife. "And she growled at him. But still, I suppose she would never grow."

"Never," agreed Dick. "She would have been cut dead by all the best dogs in New York."

"You know," said Ellen, after a time, as she began to stack up the dishes, "maybe it was because I nursed her through that sick spell. . . ." She sighed. Dick knew that sigh.

"How about running up to this chap's farm and

finding out how she's getting along?" he asked. "We wouldn't have to let her see us."

"All right," said Ellen quickly. "We could just stop and ask how she is doing and I could tell his wife about the broth and lean meat."

So one afternoon they hired the Blanchards' machine again, stopped at Eli Madden's store to ask the way to Timmons' farm, and drove up the road until they sighted his name on a gray mailbox in front of a large, rambling farmhouse.

Timmons was kneeling in a small room of the barns, sorting over some implements, when Dickinson found him.

"Hello, Timmons," he said, with a worried crease in his forehead, "I just dropped in to ask about the dog."

"Darned if Norb Gibbs didn't take her," said Timmons, rising. "He stopped up here one day and he had a little likker on him. Norb's a mean man. He's the orneriest cuss in these parts. Well, sir, your dog was runnin' 'round in front of the house and Norb took a fancy to her. I said I didn't want to sell, seein' as she'd bin give to us, and he kidded me, like, and said well, no, you wouldn't want to sell a gift dog— he'd just take her. And he did. Laughed when I tried to stop him."

"Can't you have the sheriff or someone get the dog?" asked Dick.

Josephine Has Her Day

"Sheriff's 'way off to the county seat and his deputy here is a little thick with Gibbs. Nobody ever crosses him much. He's a hard man."

With a gesture of annoyance Dickinson finally asked the farmer to say nothing of the dog's disappearance. It wouldn't do for the thing to be talked about in the village. Then he went back to rejoin his wife.

"Did you see her?" she smiled wistfully.

"No," said Dick, with a great effort at lightness. "But she's doing fine, Timmons said."

"I'm sure she is," said Mrs. Dickinson. "I've told Mrs. Timmons all about her idiosyncrasies. Well... I guess we must be getting back home. It looks a lot like rain."

And it did rain, a slow, depressing drizzle, as they returned, Dick hard put to it to affect an easy cheerfulness while his mind turned over and over the quandary into which Josephine—and he—had fallen. Perhaps it might be an easy matter to buy her back for Timmons. But how was he to arrange a meeting without his wife's knowing? Through his speculations ran alternately an undercurrent of exasperation at all this bother about an undesirable pup, a thin-lipped anger at the unknown brute's action, and a faint feeling of dread.

Schemes for recovering the puppy for Timmons kept formulating in his brain. He was still thinking of the problem when, next day, he walked to Madden's store to replenish his supply of tobacco. He decided to query the storekeeper about the haunts and habits of the unseen man who never left his thoughts.

"Norb Gibbs?" asked Madden. "Right there." He jerked his thumb.

Dickinson turned to observe a group of three men in one corner of the store, talking haltingly in low tones, two of them pulling at pipes, the third leaning idly against a counter.

"Oh, Norb!" called Madden.

Before Dickinson could arrange his thoughts or formulate a mode of procedure, one of the smokers turned slightly and looked at the storekeeper.

"Feller here wants to see you," continued Madden.

Dick felt his heart begin to beat rapidly and his hands at the fingertips became a little cold. The man who slouched over to him, scowling, was heavy and stockily set, with a great round face, scarred on one cheek. He was dressed in a corduroy suit, with leather boots laced to the knees. He was tremendously thick through the chest, and his wrists, where they showed under the sleeves, were scraggly black with hair. Dick stuffed his half-filled pipe into his pocket.

"You want me?" asked Gibbs, scratching his neck with big fingers of his right hand.

"Why—" began Dick. "I—yes. That is—you have a little dog I'd like to buy from you if I could."

"What dog?" demanded Gibbs.

"A puppy I believe you got from Mr. Timmons," said Dick with a wry attempt at a smile and a feeling that his voice was a little weak and that his tongue moved thickly.

"I got a pup from him," said Gibbs. "Yes." He planted his feet apart, put his pipe in one corner of his mouth, and pushed his hat a little from his forehead. "What about it?"

"Well," said Dickinson, "I gave him to Timmons and now he—that is—I—my wife and I believe we would like to have him—I mean *her*—back. How is she getting along?" He felt the question was a bit silly and out of place.

"Right well," drawled the big man. "I reckon she'll make me a good dog. Nope. Can't say I want to get shed of her."

"You wouldn't sell her?" asked Dick.

"Nope."

"How about fifty dollars?" Dick hazarded hopefully. The thought went through his mind that maybe Timmons would agree to help buy back the dog. He had offered to pay something for it.

"Don't need no money," said Gibbs curtly.

"I—I want the dog very much," said Dick.

"Well s'posin' you come get her," said Gibbs, his voice rising. "And when you come, come big."

He turned and looked at his companions, as if in-

viting them to enjoy the scene. They listened silently.
Madden, weighing out some nails on a scale, looked
up with lifted brows.

"I got a lot o' handy cordwood around the place I
use on them as I don't want prowlin' about," continued Gibbs. With a loud laugh he walked back and
rejoined his friends. Madden resumed weighing his
nails. Dick felt his face grow hot.

"You won't give her up, then?" he asked thickly.

"I said you come and get her," glowered Gibbs,
thumbing some tobacco into his short pipe and leaning against the counter. One of his friends moved over
and made more room for him.

"Maybe I will," said Dick. He was quivering
slightly and his legs felt strangely strained under him.

"And maybe you'll git a clout like I've had to give
yer damn dog now and again," laughed the man, brut-
ally, showing his teeth in a grin at his companions.

Things grew a little hazy in front of Dickinson—a
little hazy and red. He realized, with something like
a flash of fire in his brain, that this strange brute had
beaten his dog . . . Josephine. . . .

In two bounds he was across the room, for he was
lithe and quick, if no match for the other in strength.
Before Gibbs could remove one ankle from the other,
as he lounged against the counter—before he could
take the pipe from his hand, Dickinson struck him

full in the mouth with all the force of a long right swing.

They will talk about the fight that followed for many years to come. Gibbs, knocked to a sitting position between a bushel of potatoes and a heavy unopened barrel, was hampered by his weight and his heavy clothing, but when he got to his feet he rushed for Dickinson like an injured bull. The swoop of the oncoming giant was powerful. Dickinson turned and, in sheer fright, ran to the door. But there he suddenly whirled. With a quick, mad, desperate movement he hurled himself straight at the feet of the charging form. Not for nothing had he dived like that at football dummies in his school days, battering his body at the swinging stuffed moleskins as a member of the scrub team—the fighting scrubs. He struck the man just above the ankles.

Gibbs went toppling clumsily over him and hit the floor with a terrific crash. He fell near a newly opened box of hammers, glistening with blue steel heads and white-labeled handles. Dick rolled over and picked himself up as the man grasped a hammer and turned on his knees. His throw was wild. The hammer crashed into an unlighted lamp high above a counter, and glass tinkled sharply as the lamp swung and creaked dismally. As Gibbs staggered to his feet,

Thurber's Dogs

Dick jumped for a chair behind the large stove near one corner of the store. Apparently the man, another hammer in his hand, expected Dickinson to hide behind the stove, for he moved toward him with a triumphant leer on his lips.

But Dickinson did not hide. The fever of battle was on him. He darted out straight at his foe, swinging the chair up from the floor as he came. Gibbs, somewhat startled, brought his hammer stroke down squarely on the upturned legs of the chair, two of which caught him solidly under the arm. He swore and the hammer flew from his hand. His other hand went to an injured elbow as the chair dropped to the floor. He lurched for it, but Dick tackled him again and Gibbs went down on the upturned chair. Dick was behind him. With a well-directed shove of his foot he sent Gibbs into an even more ludicrous entanglement with the piece of furniture. After which he leaped upon him, hammering blows into the back of his head.

"Get up!" yelled Dick in a frenzy. "Get up, you dog stealer, you dog beater, you ———!"

The man struggled to a sitting posture and rubbed blood with his sleeve from a gash under his eye. Only his unusually slow movements, his handicap of heaviness, prevented him from closing with Dick before the latter got over his frenzy of yelling, while he stood above the defenseless man, his arms flailing about him.

But now the fellow was on his knees, his heavy hands flat on the floor, and Dickinson's reason returned. He lurched for a counter and began to hurl things at the slowly moving terror. He threw boxes, cans, racks—everything he could get his hands on. Grapefruit and tomatoes began to fly. A can of peaches plumped roundly into Gibbs' chest. A seed rack bounded from his shoulders as the swishing packets clattered about the floor. The scoop of nails which the awe-struck Madden had abandoned for the floor behind the counter sang a rattling song past Gibbs' ear and spattered like shot over walls and floor. But Gibbs got to his feet and, warding off more missiles with the chair, moved forward—relentless, grim, terrible. "I'll kill ye!" he grunted in spasmodic breaths. "I'll break ye in two!"

"Come on!" howled Dick, a challenge that was half wild fear, for the counter was bare of anything else to throw. He backed rapidly for the door. His feet struck the overturned box of hammers and he sat down. Madly he reached out and picked up a hammer and threw it. It went wide. Gibbs, seeing his foe on the floor before him, towered high, flung the chair against the stove with a clanging crash and rushed. And Dick's second hammer, flung with all his remaining strength and a rasping sob in his throat, struck Norb Gibbs directly over the eye. With a look of surprise, he fell to the floor in a heap.

The next thing Dickinson knew, the store was filled with people. He was aware that a hundred questions were being asked by a hundred forms moving in and out around him. Then abruptly the crowd made way for a figure that moved hurriedly through the door.

"Sheriff Griggsby! It's the sheriff!"

The crazy thought went through Dickinson's mind that this must be a movie. Then he fainted.

When he came to, he found himself firmly held in the arm of the law. His eyes widened and a question formed in his mind. Had he killed Gibbs?

"You're going to take a ride with me," said the sheriff grimly. Dick shivered. "You and me," continued the sheriff, "are going up after that female bitch now. I like a man 'll fight all hell for his dog, even if it *ain't* his."

Late one October day, when the western windows of houses were burning with orange fire, the Dickinsons stopped on a bench in Central Park and sat down. A sturdy little terrier with a sleek brown coat and very bright eyes, whose ancestry, however, would admittedly have been difficult to trace, jumped up and sat down between them.

Josephine Has Her Day

Presently a lady went by, leading in leash a handsome and well-groomed Scotch terrier, of evident aristocracy.

"There, but for the grace of Gibbs," mused Dickinson, "goes our Scotty."

His wife patted the little terrier by her side and looked after the retreating Scotty.

"Oh," she said, "it makes a good enough dog of its kind."

CHAPTER NINE

The Scotty Who Knew Too Much

S EVERAL SUMMERS AGO there was a Scotty who
went to the country for a visit. He decided that
all the farm dogs were cowards, because they were
afraid of a certain animal that had a white stripe
down its back. "You are a pussy-cat and I can lick
you," the Scotty said to the farm dog who lived in the
house where the Scotty was visiting. "I can lick the
little animal with the white stripe, too. Show him to
me."

"Don't you want to ask any questions about him?"
said the farm dog.

"Nah," said the Scotty. "*You* ask the questions."

So the farm dog took the Scotty into the woods and
showed him the white-striped animal and the Scotty

closed in on him, growling and slashing. It was all over in a moment and the Scotty lay on his back. When he came to, the farm dog said, "What happened?"

"He threw vitriol," said the Scotty, "but he never laid a glove on me."

A few days later the farm dog told the Scotty there was another animal all the farm dogs were afraid of. "Lead me to him," said the Scotty. "I can lick anything that doesn't wear horseshoes."

"Don't you want to ask any questions about him?" said the farm dog.

"Nah," said the Scotty. "Just show me where he hangs out." So the farm dog led him to a place in the woods and pointed out the little animal when he came along. "A clown," said the Scotty, "a pushover," and he closed in, leading with his left and exhibiting some mighty fancy footwork. In less than a second the Scotty was flat on his back, and when he woke up the farm dog was pulling quills out of him.

"What happened?" said the farm dog.

"He pulled a knife on me," said the Scotty, "but at least I have learned how you fight out here in the country, and now I am going to beat you up." So he closed in on the farm dog, holding his nose with one front paw to ward off the vitriol and covering his eyes with the other front paw to keep out the knives. The Scotty couldn't see his opponent and he couldn't smell

his opponent and he was so badly beaten that he had to be taken back to the city and put in a nursing home.

Moral: It is better to ask some of the questions than to know all the answers.

CHAPTER TEN

The Patient Bloodhound

IN MAY 1937, a bloodhound who lived in Wapokoneta Falls, Ohio, was put on the trail of a man suspected of a certain crime. The bloodhound followed him to Akron, Cleveland, Buffalo, Syracuse, Rochester, Albany, and New York. The Westminster dog show was going on at the time but the bloodhound couldn't get to the Garden because the man got on the first ship for Europe. The ship landed at Cherbourg and the bloodhound followed the man to Paris, Beauvais, Calais, Dover, London, Chester, Llandudno, Bettws-y-Coed, and Edinburgh, where the dog wasn't able to take in the international sheep trials. From Edinburgh, the bloodhound trailed the man to Liverpool, but since the man immediately got on a ship for New York, the dog didn't have a chance to explore the wonderful Liverpool smells.

Thurber's Dogs

In America again, the bloodhound traced the man to Teaneck, Tenafly, Nyack, and Peapack—where the dog didn't have time to run with the Peapack beagles. From Peapack the hound followed the man to Cincinnati, St. Louis, Kansas City, St. Louis, Cincinnati, Columbus, Akron, and finally back to Wapokoneta Falls. There the man was acquitted of the crime he had been followed for.

The bloodhound had developed fallen paw-pads and he was so worn out he could never again trail anything that was faster than a turtle. Furthermore, since he had gone through the world with his eyes and nose to the ground, he had missed all its beauty and excitement.

Moral: The paths of glory at least lead to the Grave, but the paths of duty, alas, may get you Nowhere.

THE HOUND

AND

THE HAT

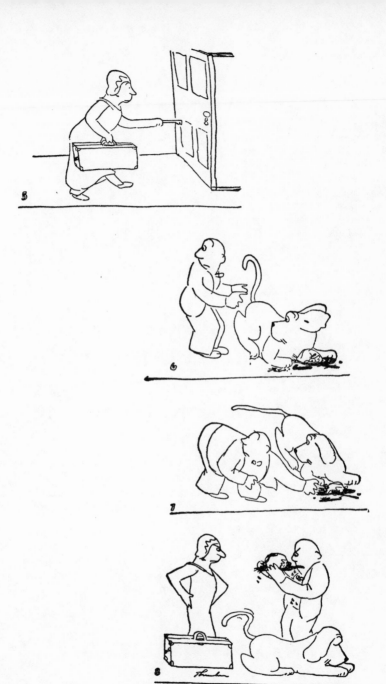

CHAPTER ELEVEN

Collie in the Driveway

ON A FINE AUGUST DAY IN 1930 one Jacob R. Ellis, of Dearborn, Michigan, vice-president of a real estate and mortgage company in Detroit, drove his car down to the corner gas station. "Fill her up, Ray, and take a look at the oil," he told the attendant. "We're off on a vacation. Going to take a swing around the East." Hundreds of thousands of men like Ellis have watched hundreds of thousands of Rays fill her up and look at the oil, and have driven off on hundreds of thousands of vacations all pretty much alike. Jacob R. Ellis' vacation of 1930 is one of the few the general public has ever read about. On his swing around the East he was destined to drive his car, in second gear, into the news columns of thousands of daily papers. He even made a front page or two in the busy and oblivious city of New York.

Thurber's Dogs

In the front seat with Mr. Ellis, who was a man of about forty then, was his son Arthur, aged fourteen, and in the back seat were Mrs. Ellis and a niece of the Ellises named Janice. Of a group so innocent and so typical it is unnecessary to draw sharp or comprehensive pictures. Mr. Ellis wears pin-stripe suits, smokes cigarettes, plays handball now and then at the club during the lunch hour; he is medium-sized, easy to talk to, knows the land-and-mortage game like a book. Arthur was at that time a blond youngster, a bit on the thin side, crazy about dogs, a great reader of *Boy's Life* and *The American Boy*. Mrs. Marguerite Ellis and her niece Janice you have vaguely noticed thousands of times in the back seat of passing cars. Nice people, average people, these four, like dozens you have known. What marks them out for our special attention is that although they didn't, of course, know it, they were on their way to kill Albert Payson Terhune's famous collie Sunnybank Jean. Maybe you remember them now. "The damned dog committed suicide," Mr. Ellis says nowadays in speaking of the painful incident, into whose ironic little pattern of tragedy we must, in fairness to both the Ellises and the Terhunes, probe as carefully and as justly as may be.

The Ellises spent several days among the monuments of Washington and then drove on to Princeton,

Collie in the Driveway

New Jersey, where they had friends. It was in Princeton that little Arthur began to pluck at his father's sleeve and insist on being taken to visit the Terhune kennels at Pompton Lakes. Mr. Terhune was by way of being an idol of Arthur's, which is to say a god, for Arthur was fourteen. Albert Payson Terhune was reputed to be able to carry on conversations with his dogs—how wonderful it would be to see, perhaps to shake hands with, such a man! Arthur had read the famous author's stories in every magazine that carried them. "He was always getting me to spend two-fifty or three dollars for the latest Terhune book, too," Mr. Ellis will tell you if you drop in at his office on the twentieth floor of a Detroit office building and are able to get him started on the subject. He doesn't like to talk about it, he says, and often has refused to; he has a way of saying he's not going to tell the story even as he goes on to tell it. Not long after the thing happened the *American Weekly* tried to interview him, but he said he wouldn't be interviewed. He was made pretty sick of the whole business as soon as he got home from the ill-fated invasion of New Jersey. Friends would call him up on the phone and say "Doggone!" or stop him in the street and say "Yah, yah, you old dog-killer!" It got pretty monotonous, Ellis says, but you know how fellas are when they start riding you about something.

Arthur's deep interest in Terhune and the Terhune

dogs had influenced his father to read some of the
books, of which Arthur had a sizable row in his
room. The elder Ellis remembers the names of several of them: *Lad: a Dog, Bugg, a Collie, Further
Adventures of Lad, Lad of Sunnybank.* "They were
pretty good," says Mr. Ellis. It was the youngster's
enthusiasm and not the father's, however, that forced
the Pompton Lakes venture. Arthur kept saying that
Mr. Terhune in his articles (Mr. Ellis refers to all
forms of prose writing as articles) invited everybody
to come and see his dogs. The Ellises certainly ought
to go since they were so near—what about it, Dad,
what do you say, Dad? Mr. Ellis made the typical
surrender of the indulgent American father. He says
he was a little dubious about Terhune's wanting
everybody to come and see his dogs, but the kid had
his heart set on it, so he thought, What the hell, let's
go, they can't kill us. They set off for Pompton Lakes
one afternoon.

The Ellises' Ford sedan arrived in the village at
6 P.M. and the elder Ellises were all for going to a
hotel and waiting till next day; but Arthur could
practically smell the air of Sunnybank and they had
to go on. "There was a large 'No Trespassing' sign on
the gates, all right," says Mr. Ellis, "but Arthur kept
telling about Terhune inviting everybody in his
articles, so I drove to the caretaker's cottage at the entrance to the place. Arthur claimed he even knew the

caretaker from the articles—felt he knew him, you know. Well, a woman stuck her head out of the cottage and I said we'd like to see the kennels. So she yells, 'People here to see the kennels,' to somebody behind some bushes, and he yells back, 'Kennels closed. Tell 'em to come back tomorrow.' Arthur was pretty cut up about being so close and not getting in, but I said we'd try it again next day."

The next morning, Mr. Ellis remembers, was bright and beautiful, as fine a morning as you'd want to see. Arthur had his father up early and the Ellises were off again long before noon. There was the same ritual at the caretaker's lodge, except that this time the voice from the bushes said, "Tell 'em to go in." The roadway was winding and its gravel was damp. Mr. Ellis decided to take it in second. "I'm a good and careful driver," he says. "You can look up my record." What happened next happened so fast and plunged everybody into the depths of so great an emotional scene that historicity was shattered by the impact and only the fragments of legend are left. The driveway was lined with trees and bushes and out of them suddenly, as Ellis remembers it, came a tan flash, and there was a dull, heavy sound as the moving body hit the radiator of the car. Ellis stopped the car instantly and got out. There lay Sunnybank Jean. "She didn't even whimper," says Ellis. "All there was was her banging into the radiator. Just below the

cap." It is at this point in the narrative that he sometimes insists the collie committed suicide. It seemed
like that to Jacob Ellis, a good and careful driver,
proceeding in second gear up a strange, winding
driveway, naturally on the alert. It did not seem like
that to Albert Payson Terhune, who appeared
through the trees and bushes as suddenly and wildly
as the collie had. He burst into a flaming rage. "He
said some terrible things to us," says Jacob Ellis. "He
called us vandals and barbarians and trippers and
tourists—things like that. He kept screaming like
mad and shouting for the caretaker to get the police.
He said he'd have us up. He said we'd pay for this."

The confused and passionate scene, as recon-
structed by the newspapers, failed to do any justice
at all to perhaps its most tragic figure, that of Arthur
Ellis, collie-lover, Terhune-worshipper, abruptly
brought face to face with two of his cherished idols,
one dead by his father's car, the other demoniacal
with rage against all Ellises. Probably nobody paid
much attention to the little boy. His father remembers that Arthur was out of the car and bending over
the dog when Terhune crashed into the picture. We
toss the moment to the fiction writers: one school will
find a sharp note of anguish in the tableau of the boy
and the dog and the shattered, raging idol; another

may tinker with the coldly pleasurable excitement that the very young are said to derive from the heart of calamity. To both schools it is only fair to report that when Arthur was being driven away from the scene he said finally, to his father, "You know what, Dad? We ought've punched that guy in the nose." Mr. Terhune lost more than a dog that day, he lost a devoted reader. When Arthur got back to Dearborn he took all his Terhune books and carried them to the attic. "He never said anything," says his father, "he just took them to the attic." They are still there. Mr. Ellis says that his son also gave up his interest in dogs. "He turned his attention to mechanics—steam engines, things like that."

We must go back to the driveway, however, for we are ahead of our story. While Mr. Terhune fulminated, someone—Ellis says it was Mrs. Terhune—tried to force some liquor from a bottle into the dog's mouth, but it was no use. Sunnybank Jean was dead. She was thirteen years old, and that is a long time for anyone to have a dog; and she had been a good dog, even a famous dog. Jacob Ellis has his moments when he understands the fury that descended on the owner of Sunnybank Jean, who faced in his driveway a group of strange, uninvited people from Detroit who had killed his beloved pet. But if the owner was heartbroken, the visitors were profoundly shaken. "It ruined our vacation," says Mr. Ellis. "On the way home none of us mentioned it and there wasn't a word out of Arthur after what he said about punching Terhune in the nose. I knew how he felt and I left him alone. I wasn't mad at Terhune then, and I'm not now. Maybe I would have acted the same way if it had been my dog."

Terhune had all the Ellises up before a justice of the peace, and that before Jean's body was cold. The caretaker had called the state police and a state policeman arrived quickly. Mr. Ellis remembers him as big and calm, a rock of comfort in the tumultuous sea of emotion. Terhune told the policeman he wanted the Ellises charged with malicious mischief, reckless driving, trespassing, property damages, and some other things Mr. Ellis has forgotten. The cop said O. K. He quietly told Ellis to drive on back to town and he would follow. "You go first," said Ellis. "I don't want to kill any more dogs." "O. K.," said the cop. They drove to the office of a Justice Dawes in a building housing a bank and a real-estate office. Terhune, who had gone for his lawyer, reappeared with him, signed the papers of complaint, and stormed out of the office. Arthur must have looked stricken and miserable in the midst of his first experience with the law. The justice patted him on the shoulder and, ac-

Collie in the Driveway

cording to Mr. Ellis, said, "Don't mind, sonny. Idols often have feet of clay." The story had spread around town and the Ellises were not without sympathizers. One or two hangers-on around the court told Ellis that Terhune had been mighty uppity lately. Seems he had gone into a local movie house one night and when he saw some of the men in the audience were in their shirt sleeves he stood up during the intermission and bawled them out—gave 'em hell, said they ought to be ashamed of themselves. This was somehow comforting to Jacob Ellis.

The Ellises had not seen the last of the formidable dog man. He came back into the courtroom the way they had first seen him come through the trees of the driveway, like summer thunder, and announced that the dog was worth five hundred dollars and he wanted the trippers to pay that much for what they had done; he would give the money to the police retirement fund. "I thought five hundred dollars was a pretty long price for a thirteen-year-old dog," says Ellis, "and the judge and Terhune's attorney seemed to agree with me. The judge dismissed all the charges finally except the property-destruction one, and it was decided I should pay a hundred dollars. I only had eighty-five on me, to get home with, and had to wire my office for the hundred." It was three o'clock in the afternoon before the money came through.

Thurber's Dogs

Ellis gave it to Justice Dawes and the family got into their car and headed for Detroit.

Arthur Ellis, the boy who wanted to see the Sunnybank dogs and shake hands with the great Albert Payson Terhune, must be going on forty now. I have no report from anyone who has ever talked to him about the tragedy that got him into the newspapers and the courts, made him put his dog books in the attic and turn to mechanics. Probably his desire to punch Albert Payson Terhune in the nose is as dead as the whole story. It was tossed rather helter-skelter into the newspapers and died there in a rather awkward position. I have tried here to arrange its limbs a little more decorously, and to close its eyes.

CHAPTER TWELVE

The Departure of Emma Inch

EMMA INCH looked no different from any other middle-aged, thin woman you might glance at in the subway or deal with across the counter of some small store in a country town, and then forget forever. Her hair was drab and unabundant, her face made no impression on you, her voice I don't remember—it was just a voice. She came to us with a letter of recommendation from some acquaintance who knew that we were going to Martha's Vineyard for the summer and wanted a cook. We took her because there was nobody else, and she seemed all right. She had arrived at our hotel in Forty-fifth Street the day before we were going to leave and we got her a room for the night, because she lived way uptown somewhere. She said she really ought to go back and give up her room, but I told her I'd fix that.

Thurber's Dogs

Emma Inch had a big scuffed brown suitcase with her, and a Boston bull terrier. His name was Feely. Feely was seventeen years old and he grumbled and growled and snuffled all the time, but we needed a cook and we agreed to take Feely along with Emma Inch, if she would take care of him and keep him out of the way. It turned out to be easy to keep Feely out of the way because he would lie grousing anywhere Emma put him until she came and picked him up again. I never saw him walk. Emma had owned him, she said, since he was a pup. He was all she had in the world, she told us, with a mist in her eyes. I felt embarrassed but not touched. I didn't see how anybody could love Feely.

I didn't lose any sleep about Emma Inch and Feely the night of the day they arrived, but my wife did. She told me next morning that she had lain awake a long time thinking about the cook and her dog, because she felt kind of funny about them. She didn't know why. She just had a feeling that they were kind of funny. When we were all ready to leave—it was about three o'clock in the afternoon, for we had kept putting off the packing—I phoned Emma's room, but she didn't answer. It was getting late and we felt nervous—the Fall River boat would sail in about two hours. We couldn't understand why we hadn't heard anything from Emma and Feely. It wasn't until four o'clock that we did. There was a small rap on the door

of our bedroom and I opened it and Emma and Feely were there, Feely in her arms, snuffling and snaffling, as if he had been swimming a long way.

My wife told Emma to get her bag packed, we were leaving in a little while. Emma said her bag *was* packed, except for her electric fan, and she couldn't get that in. "You won't need an electric fan at the Vineyard," my wife told her. "It's cool there, even during the day, and it's almost cold at night. Besides, there is no electricity in the cottage we are going to."

Emma Inch seemed distressed. She studied my wife's face. "I'll have to think of something else then," she said. "Mebbe I could let the water run all night."

We both sat down and looked at her. Feely's asthmatic noises were the only sounds in the room for a while. "Doesn't that dog ever stop that?" I asked, irritably.

"Oh, he's just talking," said Emma. "He talks all the time, but I'll keep him in my room and he won't bother you none."

"Doesn't he bother you?" I asked.

"He *would* bother me," said Emma, "at night, but I put the electric fan on and keep the light burning. He don't make so much noise when it's light, because he don't snore. The fan kind of keeps me from noticing him. I put a piece of cardboard, like, where the fan hits it and then I don't notice Feely so much.

The Departure of Emma Inch

Mebbe I could let the water run in my room all night instead of the fan."

I said "Hmmm" and got up and mixed a drink for my wife and me—we had decided not to have one till we got on the boat, but I thought we'd better have one now. My wife didn't tell Emma there would be no running water in her room at the Vineyard.

"We've been worried about you, Emma," I said. "I phoned your room but you didn't answer."

"I never answer the phone," said Emma, "because I always get a shock. I wasn't there anyways. I couldn't sleep in that room. I went back to Mrs. Mc-Coy's on Seventy-eighth Street."

I lowered my glass. "You went back to Seventy-eighth Street last *night?*" I demanded.

"Yes, sir," she said. "I had to tell Mrs. McCoy I was going away and wouldn't be there any more for a while—Mrs. McCoy's the landlady. Anyways, I never sleep in a hotel." She looked around the room. "They burn down," she told us.

It came out that Emma Inch had not only gone back to Seventy-eighth Street the night before but had walked all the way, carrying Feely. It had taken her an hour or two, because Feely didn't like to be carried very far at a time, so she had had to stop every block or so and put him down on the sidewalk for a while. It had taken her just as long to walk back to our hotel, too; Feely, it seems, never got up before afternoon—that's why she was so late. She was sorry. My wife and I finished our drinks, looking at each other, and at Feely.

Emma Inch didn't like the idea of riding to Pier 14 in a taxi, but after ten minutes of cajoling and pleading she finally got in. "Make it go slow," she said. We had enough time, so I asked the driver to take it easy. Emma kept getting to her feet and I kept pulling her back onto the seat.

"I never been in an automobile before," she said. "It goes awful fast." Now and then she gave a little squeal of fright.

The driver turned his head and grinned. "You're O.K. wit' me, lady," he said. Feely growled at him.

Emma waited until he had turned away again, and then she leaned over to my wife and whispered. "They all take cocaine," she said. Feely began to make a new sound—a kind of high, agonized yelp. "He's singing," said Emma. She gave a strange little giggle, but the expression of her face didn't change.

"I wish you had put the Scotch where we could get at it," said my wife.

If Emma Inch had been afraid of the taxicab, she was terrified by the *Priscilla* of the Fall River Line. "I don't think I can go," said Emma. "I don't think I could get on a boat. I didn't know they were so big." She stood rooted to the pier, clasping Feely. She must have squeezed him too hard, for he screamed—

The Departure of Emma Inch

he screamed like a woman. We all jumped. "It's his ears," said Emma. "His ears hurt." We finally got her on the boat, and once aboard, in the salon, her terror abated somewhat. Then the three parting blasts of the boat whistle rocked lower Manhattan. Emma Inch leaped to her feet and began to run, letting go of her suitcase (which she had refused to give up to a porter) but holding on to Feely. I caught her just as she reached the gangplank. The ship was on its way when I let go of her arm.

It was a long time before I could get Emma to go to her stateroom, but she went at last. It was an inside stateroom, and she didn't seem to mind it. I think she was surprised to find that it was like a room, and had a bed and a chair and a washbowl. She put Feely down on the floor. "I think you'll have to do something about the dog," I said. "I think they put them somewhere and you get them when you get off."

"No, they don't," said Emma.

I guess, in this case, they didn't. I don't know. I shut the door on Emma Inch and Feely, and went away. My wife was drinking straight Scotch when I got to our stateroom.

The next morning, cold and early, we got Emma and Feely off the *Priscilla* at Fall River and over to New Bedford in a taxi and onto the little boat for Martha's Vineyard. Each move was as difficult as

getting a combative drunken man out of the night club
in which he fancies he has been insulted. Emma sat in
a chair on the Vineyard boat, as far away from sight
of the water as she could get, and closed her eyes and
held on to Feely. She had thrown a coat over Feely,
not only to keep him warm, but to prevent any of the
ship's officers from taking him away from her. I went
in from the deck at intervals to see how she was. She
was all right, or at least all right for her, until the
only stop between New Bedford and the Vineyard.
Then Feely got sick. Or at any rate Emma said he was
sick. There were tears in her eyes. "He's a very sick
dog, Mr. Thurman," she said. "I'll have to take him
home." I knew by the way she said "home" what she
meant. She meant Seventy-eighth Street.

The boat tied up at Woods Hole and was motion-
less and we could hear the racket of the deckhands on
the dock loading freight. "I'll get off here," said
Emma firmly, or with more firmness, anyway, than
she had shown yet. I explained to her that we would
be home in half an hour, that everything would be
fine then, everything would be wonderful. I said
Feely would be a new dog. I told her people sent sick
dogs to Martha's Vineyard to be cured. But it was
no good. "I'll have to take him off here," said Emma.
"I always have to take him home when he is sick." I
talked to her eloquently about the loveliness of
Martha's Vineyard and the nice houses and the nice

The Departure of Emma Inch

people and the wonderful accommodations for dogs. But I knew it was useless. I could tell by looking at her. She was going to get off the boat at Woods Hole.

"You really can't do this," I said, grimly, shaking her arm. Feely snarled weakly. "You haven't any money and you don't know where you are. You're a long way from New York. Nobody ever got from Woods Hole to New York alone." She didn't seem to hear me. She began walking toward the stairs leading to the gangplank, crooning to Feely. "You'll have to go all the way back on boats," I said, "or else take a train, and you haven't any money."

"I don't want any money, Mr. Thurman," she said. "I haven't earned any money."

I walked along in irritable silence for a moment; then I gave her some money. I made her take it. We got to the gangplank. Feely snaffled and gurgled. I saw now that his eyes were a little red and moist. I knew it would do no good to summon my wife—not when Feely's health was at stake. "How do you expect to get home from here?" I almost shouted at Emma Inch as she moved down the gangplank. "You're way out on the end of Massachusetts."

She stopped and turned around. "We'll walk," she said. "We like to walk, Feely and me." I just stood and watched her go.

When I went up on deck, the boat was clearing for the Vineyard. "How's everything?" asked my wife.

Thurber's Dogs

I waved a hand in the direction of the dock. Emma Inch was standing there, her suitcase at her feet, her dog under one arm, waving good-by to us with her free hand. I had never seen her smile before, but she was smiling now.

CHAPTER THIRTEEN

The Thin Red Leash

IT TAKES COURAGE for a tall thin man to lead a tiny
Scotch terrier pup on a smart red leash in our
neighborhood, that region bounded roughly (and
how!) by Hudson and West Streets, where the Village takes off its Windsor tie and dons its stevedore
corduroys. Here men are guys and all dogs are part
bull. Here "cute" apartments stand quivering like
pioneers on the prairie edge.

The first day that I sallied forth with Black Watch
III bounding tinily at the street end of the thin red
leash, a cement finisher, one of the crowd that finds
an esoteric pleasure in standing on the bleak corner of
Hudson and Horatio Streets, sat down on the sidewalk and guffawed. There were hoots and whistles.

It was apparent that the staunch and plucky Scotch
terrier breed was, to these uninitiated bulldog-lovers,

the same as a Pekingese. But Black Watch must have his airing. So I continued to brave such witticisms as "Hey, fella, where's the rest of it?" and—this from a huge steamfitter—"What d'y' say me an' you an' the dog go somewheres and have tea?"

Once a dockworker demanded, in a tone indicating he would not take Black Watch III for an answer, "What's that thing's name?"

My courage failed me. "Mike," I said, giving the leash a red-blooded jerk and cursing the Scotty. The whole affair was a challenge to my gumption. I had been scared to call my dog by its right name.

The gang was on hand in full force the next evening. One of them snapped enormous calloused fingers at Black Watch and he bounded away, leash and all, from my grasp.

"Black Watch!" I shouted—if you could call it shouting.

"What did y' call that dog, fella?" demanded a man who, I think, blows through truck exhaust whistles to test them.

"Black Watch," said I.

"What's that mean?" he asked menacingly.

"It was a Scottish regiment wiped out at Ypres or somewhere," I said, pronouncing it "Eeprr."

"Wiped out where?" he snarled.

"Wiped out at Wipers," I said.

"That's better," he said.

The Thin Red Leash

I again realized that I had shown the white feather. That night I took a solemn, if not fervent, oath to tell the next heavy-footed lout that flayed my dog to go to hell. The following evening the gang was more numerous than ever. A gigantic chap lunged forward at us. He had the build of a smokestack-wrecker.

"Psst!" he hissed. Black Watch held his ground.

"They're scrappers, these dogs," I protested amiably.

"What d' they scrap—cockroaches?" asked another man, amid general laughter. I realized that now was the time to die. After all, there are certain slurs that you can't take about your dog—gang or no gang. Just then a monstrous man, evidently a former Hudson Duster who lifts locomotives from track to track when the turntables are out of order, lounged out of a doorway.

"Whadda we got here?" he growled.

"Park Avenoo pooch," sneered one gas-house gangster. The train-lifter eyed Black Watch, who was wagging his tail in a most friendly manner.

"Scotty, ain't it?" asked the train-lifter, producing a sack of scrap tobacco.

"Yeah," I said, as easily as I could.

"Damn fine dogs, Scotties," said the train-lifter. "You gotta good 'un there, when it puts on some age, scout. Hellcats in a fight, too, *I* mean. Seen one take the tonsils out of a Airedale one day."

"Yeah?" asked the smokestack-wrecker.

"Yeah," said the train-lifter.

"Yeah," said I.

Several huge hands went down to pat a delighted shaggy head. There were no more catcalls or hoots. Black Watch III had been acquitted of Pomeranianism. We're quite good friends now, Black Watch and the gang and I. They call him Blackie. I am grateful to a kind Fate that had given the train-lifter the chance, between carrying locomotives, to see a Scotty in action.

CHAPTER FOURTEEN

In Defense of Dogs, Even, After a Fashion, Jeannie

WHILE DIGGING UP, for this rambling treatise, some fugitive things I had written about dogs but never preserved, I turned an old lost corner one day and came upon two ancient and conflicting pieces of indignation. One of these was a woozily implemented attack on dogs, written by Stanley Walker twenty years ago for a now dead magazine called *For Men,* and the other was a singularly persuasive and curiously moving defense of dogs, written, for a subsequent issue of the same magazine, by me. I take that last part back. I should like to be able to report that I was a skilful controversialist in those vital years, with a deceptively ingratiating courtroom manner, apt quotations from Shelley and the Bible at my fingertips, and a faint, fleeting smile playing about the corners of my inscrutable mouth, but the truth is that time has tarnished and diminished what my learned opponent and I had to say. We both used unfair tactics, pure guesswork, and what still has the ring of downright prevarication. I trust that our readers forgave us our hot-blooded impetuosity, if we had any readers. I never heard from one.

My gifted colleague's strategy consisted mainly of adducing dubious evidence of the tendency of dogs to break up the emotional relationships of men and women. He cited the case of a standard poodle that a gentleman caller filled full of brandy while his girl friend, the dog's owner, was upstairs dressing. When she finally descended, her eyes flashed lightning, for hell hath no fury like that of a lady whose dog has been debauched, and she threw her suitor out of her house and her life. The strangest exhibit offered in evidence by the prosecution, with dazzling dexterity, was the story of another gentleman caller who sat down on his sweetheart's dog, ruining the evening, frightening the neighbors, killing the dog, and terminating the love affair. Mr. Walker, with devilish cunning, suggested to the jury that the late dog was solely responsible for its own death and for the end of the affair.

I have no desire to revive the whole yellowing record of our forgotten debate, for I feel that oblivion

In Defense of Dogs

has mercifully descended upon the back files of *For Men,* but I should like to freshen and repeat my reply to one of Mr. Walker's old indictments. "The history of the dog," he said without batting an eye, "is one of greed, double-crossing, and unspeakable lechery." I submitted then, and I resubmit, that if you stopped ten persons on the street and asked them, "The history of what species is one of greed, double-crossing, and unspeakable lechery," six would promptly reply, "Man," three would walk on hastily without a word, and one would call the police. (Two or more would probably call the police nowadays, but the point is unimportant.)

My inherent fairness and open mind led me to admit that some dogs have been known to let people down, or stand them up, or exasperate and even distress them by unpredictable behavior. I even went so far as to confess that some of my own dogs had double-crossed me for a total, as I put it then, of sixteen or eighteen times, but I quickly added that the basic fault was, in almost every instance, my own. There were, for special examples, certain unhelpful activities of Jeannie, the Scotch terrier I owned from 1926 to 1933.

In a 1936 piece called "The Admiral on the Wheel" I recalled what Jeannie had done to me one day ten years before: "When the colored maid stepped on my glasses the other morning, it was the

first time they had been broken since the late Thomas
A. Edison's seventy-ninth birthday. I remember that
day well, because I was working for a newspaper then
and I had been assigned to go over to West Orange
that morning and interview Mr. Edison. I got up
early, and, in reaching for my glasses under the bed
(where I always put them), I found that Jeannie was
quietly chewing them. Both tortoise-shell temples
(the pieces that go over your ears) had been eaten and
Jeannie was toying with the lenses in a sort of jaded
way." Under the bed is no place for glasses. If I had
put them on the dresser, Jeannie would never have
eaten them, mainly, of course, because she couldn't
reach that high, but that is beside the point.

It was neither Jeannie's fault nor mine that she embarrassed me beyond measure, about a year later, at
the corner of Fifth Avenue and Eleventh Street,
where she gave birth to the unexpected fifth and last
of her first litter of puppies. She had begun having the
pups at the ungodly hour of six A.M., in a shoe closet.
It was a narrow and dark and cluttered closet, and
only a female in love with chaos, or on her way back
to the womb of confusion, would have selected such
a place. She seemed to know less about having puppies than I did—but that is a story which would interest only a veterinarian. It was nearly three hours
later, or just when the city was going to work, that the
fifth pup made her appearance. I had been taking the

mother dog for a walk, which both of us needed. I had a headache as the result of having had too much to drink the night before and not enough sleep. Quite a crowd gathered, which did not seem to bother Jeannie, but it bothered me. I put the newcomer in my pocket, told the loudly protesting mother to shut up, and hurried home, which was mercifully less than a block away, at 65 West Eleventh. This, as I have admitted, was neither Jeannie's fault nor mine, but the case of the large portion of apple cake was as much my fault as the glasses under the bed. Mr. Walker would damn me as a sentimentalist for taking the blame, but let us all be as calm as we can while I narrate exactly what happened.

I was living, at the time, in a house at Sneden's Landing on the Hudson. Jeannie and her five pups lived in a pen in the dining room. It would take too long to explain why. The only other person in the house besides me was an Italian cook named Josephine. I used to come out to the house from New York every night by train, arriving just in time for dinner. One evening, worrying about some impending disaster, or dreaming about some old one, I was carried past my station—all the way to Haverstraw, where I had to wait two hours for a train to take me back. I telephoned Josephine from Haverstraw and told her I would not be able to get there until ten o'clock. She was pretty much put out, but she said she would keep dinner for me. An hour before the train arrived to take me back, I got so hungry that I ate two sandwiches and drank two cups of coffee. Naturally when I got home finally and sat down at the dining-room table, I had no stomach at all for the wonderful dinner Josephine had kept for me. I ate the soup, but I couldn't touch any of the steak. When Josephine set it down before me I said "Wonderful!" in feigned delight and as soon as she went back into the kitchen, I cut it up and fed it to Jeannie. We got away with it fine. Josephine was pleased to see my plate licked clean. It looked as if everything was going to be all right, when Josephine suddenly set in front of me the largest piece of apple cake I had ever seen. I knew how Josephine prided herself on her cake, but I couldn't eat any of it. So when she went out to the kitchen for the coffee I handed Jeannie the apple cake, hurried to the door which opened from the dining room into the backyard, and put her out, cake and all. Josephine was in high spirits when she saw with what dispatch and evident relish I had disposed of her pastry. It was while I was in the midst of a long and flowery series of compliments on her marvelously light hand with pastry that there came a scratching at the door. Josephine went over and opened it. In trotted Jeannie, still carrying the apple cake.

Now it is my contention (although it wasn't at the time) that I double-crossed Jeannie as much as she double-crossed me. After all, I had filled her with steak (she had already had her dinner) and then asked her to consume an enormous slice of apple cake. She was only about a foot and a half long and it was too much for her. I should have known this. But, you will ask, why didn't she bury it, for God's sake? And why, I will ask you, should she have? Dogs are trained to take and carry whatever you hand them that isn't edible, and they are not supposed to go and hide it somewhere. To Scotch terriers apple cake is not edible. Jeannie had no way of knowing how profoundly she was embarrassing me. A French poodle would have sensed the delicacy of the situation that was bound to develop between me and Josephine when the apple cake rematerialized. Josephine's French was much better than her English, and this had made it hard for me to explain to her, over the phone, what I was doing in Haverstraw. I had finally told her, in uneasy French, "I have disappeared for two hours. I am sad. Good morning." And I had hung up.

Josephine had an extraordinary fondness for Jeannie and her five pups, and her affection blandly survived the night, two months later, when the dining room became flooded with several inches of river water, a nocturnal disaster that the pups turned into a carnival. Josephine was finally aroused by a strange clatter belowstairs. She went down to discover the puppies having a wonderful time. They were not only splashing about in the water, but they had managed to launch various craft and were jumping in and out of a wooden salad bowl and other objects they had dragged into the water. Josephine later described the scene, in English, like this: "Dey laugh! Dey cry! Dey sing! Dey so happy!" Jeannie was bored by the water festival, and was lying on a broad window sill, licking her wet feet. I do not blame this night's happenings on her or anybody else, but she was certainly to blame for what happened when I took her to Columbus, Ohio, one summer on vacation.

Jeannie disappeared one morning from the home of friends my wife and I were visiting. Two days later I reported the disappearance to my old friend Harry E French, then chief of the Columbus police department, and he assigned two detectives, whom I shall call Burke and Scanlon, to the case. I can't remember now who suggested the theory that foul play, or petty larceny, might be involved. It couldn't have been me, because I knew that Jeannie was a strayer, and it was getting harder and harder for me to conceive of anybody deliberately wanting to own her. Anyway, the detectives took over, but they let me ride with them in a squad car to the home of an ancient white-haired colored man whose seventeen children and fifty-six grandchildren were said by the detectives to be responsible for various disappearances in Columbus, of both the sentient and the insentient. It seemed that one of the grandsons collected refuse in the neighborhood of my host and hostess. The detectives ransacked the old man's house, and appeared to be familiar with every room and every nook and cranny. The old man did not rise from his rocking chair, but kept beating on the floor with his cane and shouting, "Heah! Heah! Heah!" There was something ritualistic about the whole thing. I found myself taking sides suddenly, as if I were assuming a role in a municipal pageant. I liked the old man, and began finding fault with the methods of Burke and Scanlon, and rearranging things they had disarranged. They were monosyllabic, gum-chewing detectives and didn't seem to be on anybody's side, even each other's.

"There isn't any Scotty here," I announced finally, as they stared at me without interest, chewing slowly. "If the dog does show up," I heard myself blurt out to the old man, "you can have it."

He banged his cane and hollered, "No, no, no!" Burke and Scanlon watched us both, not narrowly, just watched, for a few moments; then they shrugged in unison and went away.

I found Jeannie two days later, through an ad in the Columbus *Dispatch*. She was staying with some people a few houses down the block from us and they brought her home. "She acted as if she didn't belong to anybody," said the husband.

"She seemed lost and dazed," said his wife.

Before they left I put a five-dollar bill in an envelope and sealed it, and asked them if they would mind seeing that it got to their refuse collector's grandfather. They stared at me with considerably more interest than Burke and Scanlon had shown at any time, and said they certainly would, and backed away and went home.

Jeannie, as I have mentioned, was a strayer, and I once wrote a monograph about her wanderings, with some reference to the subject of roving dogs in general. I have exhumed that monograph, and it follows hereinafter, for the information and guidance of such readers as have not already had enough of Jeannieana.

CHAPTER FIFTEEN

Look Homeward, Jeannie

THE MOOT and momentous question as to whether some lost dogs have the mysterious power of being able to get back home from distant places over strange terrain has been argued for years by dog-owners, dog-haters, and other persons who know nothing whatever about dogs. Mr. Bergen Evans in his book, *The Natural History of Nonsense,* sides with the cynics who believe that the lost dog doesn't have any more idea where he is than a babe in the wood. (Author's note, 1955: I have come, somewhat reluctantly, to agree with Mr. Evans in almost all, but not quite all, cases.) "Like pigeons," Mr. Evans wrote, "dogs are thought to have a supernatural ability to find their way home across hundreds, even thousands, of miles of strange terrain. The newspapers are full of stories of dogs who have miraculously turned

up at the doorsteps of baffled masters who had abandoned them afar. Against these stories, however, can
be set the lost and found columns of the same papers,
which in almost every issue carry offers of rewards for
the recovery of dogs that, apparently, couldn't find
their way back from the next block."

Now I don't actually have any empirical knowledge of the dogs that are supposed to have returned
from strange, distant places as surely as an Indian
scout or a locomotive engineer, but I am not quite
fully prepared to write *all* of them off as figures of
pure legend. Skepticism is a useful tool of the inquisi-
tive mind, but it is scarcely a method of investigation.
I would like to see a trained reporter or private investigator set out on the trail of the homing dog and
see what he would find.

I happen to have a few haphazard clippings on the
fascinating subject, but they are unsupported, as always, by convincing proof of any kind, one way or
the other. The most interesting case is that of Bosco,
a small dog who is reported to have returned to his
house in Knoxville, Tennessee, in the winter of 1944
from Glendale, California, thus setting what is probably the world's distance record for the legendary
event, twenty-three hundred miles in seven months.
His story is recorded in a book called *Just a Mutt* by
Eldon Roark, a columnist on the Memphis *Press-
Scimitar*. Mr. Roark relates that he got his tip on the

Look Homeward, Jeannie

story from Bert Vincent of the Knoxville *News-Sentinel,* but in a letter to me Mr. Vincent wrote that he had some doubts of the truth of the long trek through towns and cities and over rivers and deserts.

Bosco belonged to a family named Flanigan, and Mr. Vincent does not question the sincerity of their belief that the dog that turned up on their porch one day was, in fact, Bosco come home. The dog bore no collar or license, however, and identification had to be made on the tricky basis of markings and behavior. The long-distance record of Bosco must be finally set down as a case that would stand up only, if I may be permitted the expression, in a court of lore.

Thurber's Dogs

Far-traveling dogs have become so common that jaded editors are inclined to turn their activities over to the society editors, and we may expect before long to encounter such items as this: "Rover, a bull terrier, owned by Mr. and Mrs. Charles L. Thompson of this city, returned to his home at 2334 Maybury Avenue yesterday, after a four-months' trip from Florida where he was lost last February. Mr. and Mrs. Thompson's daughter Alice Louise is expected home tomorrow from Shipley, to spend the summer vacation."

Incidentally, and just for the sake of a fair record, my two most recent clippings on the Long Trek deal with cats: Kit-Kat, Lake Tahoe to Long Beach, California, 525 miles; Mr. Black, Stamford, Connecticut to Atlanta, Georgia, 1,000 miles.

The homing dog reached apotheosis some years ago when the movie *Lassie Come Home* portrayed a collie returning to its young master over miles of wild and unfamiliar country in darkness and in storm. This million-dollar testament of faith, a kind of unconscious memorial to the late Albert Payson Terhune, may possibly be what inspired Bergen Evans' essay.

In the case of the "lost" dog in the next block, however, I suspect that he is on somewhat insecure ground. He assumes that the dog does not come back from the next block because it can't find its way. If this reasoning were applied to the thousands of men

Look Homeward, Jeannie

who disappear from their homes every year, it would exonerate them of every flaw except disorientation, and this is too facile an explanation for man or beast. Prince, the dog, may have just as many reasons for getting and staying the hell out as George, the husband: an attractive female, merry companions, change of routine, words of praise, small attentions, new horizons, an easing of discipline. The dog that does not come home is too large a field of research for one investigator, and so I will confine myself to the case history of Jeannie.

Jeannie had no show points to speak of. Her jaw was skimpy, her haunches frail, her forelegs slightly bowed. She thought dimly, and her co-ordination was only fair. Even in repose she had the strained, uncomfortable appearance of a woman on a bicycle.

Jeannie adjusted slowly and reluctantly to everything, including weather. Rain was a hand raised against her personally, snow a portent of evil, thunder the end of the world. She sniffed even the balmiest breeze with an air of apprehension, as if it warned of the approach of a monster at least as large as a bus.

Jeannie did everything the hard way, digging with one paw at a time, shoving out of screen doors sideways. When she was six months old, she tried to bury a bone in the second section of *The New York Times,* pushing confidently and futilely at the newsprint with her muzzle. She developed a persistent, troubled frown, which gave her the expression of someone who is trying to repair a watch with his gloves on.

Jeannie spent the first two years of her life in the city, where her outdoor experiences were confined to trips around the block. When she was taken to the country to live, she clung to the hearth for several weeks, poking her nose out now and then for a dismaying sniff of what she conceived to be God's great Scotty trap. The scent of lawn moles and the scurry of squirrels brought her out in the yard finally for tentative explorations, but it was a long time before she followed the woodchuck's trail up to the edge of the woods.

Within a few months Jeannie took to leaving the house when the sun came up and returning when it began to get dark. Her outings seemed to be good for her. She began to look sleek, fat, smug, and at the same time pleasantly puzzled, like a woman who finds more money in her handbag than she thought was there. I decided to follow her discreetly one day, and she led me a difficult two-mile chase to where a large group of summer people occupied a row of cottages near a lake. Jeannie, it came out, was the camp mascot. She had muzzled in, and for some time had been spending her days shaking down the cottagers for hamburgers, fried potatoes, cake, and marshmallows. They wondered where the cute little dog came from in the morning and where she went at night.

Look Homeward, Jeannie

Jeannie had won them over with her only trick. She could sit up, not easily, but with amusing effort, placing her right forefoot on a log or stone, and pushing. Her sitting-up stance was teetery and precarious, but if she fell over on her back or side, she was rewarded just the same, if not, indeed, even more bountifully. She couldn't lose. The camp was a pushover.

Little old One Trick had a slow mind, but she gradually figured out that the long trip home after her orgies was a waste of time, an unnecessary loop in her new economy. Oh, she knew the way back all right —by what improbable system of landmarks I could never guess—but when she got home there was no payoff except a plain wholesome meal once a day. That was all right for young dogs and very old dogs and spaniels, but not for a terrier who had struck it rich over the hills. She took to staying away for days at a time. I would have to go and get her in the car and bring her back.

One day, the summer people, out for a hike, brought her home themselves, and Jeannie realized the game was up, for the campers obviously believed in what was, to her, the outworn principle of legal ownership. To her dismay they showed themselves to be believers in one-man loyalty, a virtue which Jeannie had outgrown. The next time I drove to the camp to get her she wasn't there. I found out finally from the man who delivered the mail where she had gone.

Thurber's Dogs

"Your little dog is on the other side of the lake," he said. "She's stayin' with a schoolteacher in a cottage the other side of the lake." I found her easily enough.

The schoolteacher had opened her door one morning to discover a small Scotty sitting up in the front yard, begging. The cute little visitor had proceeded to take her new hostess for three meals a day, topped off now and then with chocolates. But I had located her hiding place, and the next time she disappeared from home she moved on to fresh fields. "Your little dog's stayin' with some folks over near Danbury," the mailman told me a week later. He explained how to get to the house. "The hell with it," I said, but a few hours later I got in the car and went after her, anyway.

She was lying on the front porch of her current home in a posture of truculent possession. When I stopped the car at the curb she charged vociferously down the steps, not to greet the master, but to challenge a trespasser. When she got close enough to recognize me, her belligerence sagged. "Better luck next time," I said, coldly. I opened the door and she climbed slowly into the car and up onto the seat beside me. We both stared straight ahead all the way home.

Jeannie was a lost dog, lost in another way than Bergen Evans realizes. There wasn't anything to do about it. After all, I had my own life to live. Before long I would have had to follow her as far as Stamford or Darien or wherever the gravy happened to be thickest and the clover sweetest. "Your little dog—" the mailman began a few days later.

"I know," I said. "Thanks," and went back into the house. She came home of her own accord about three weeks later, and I think she actually made an effort to adjust herself. It was too late, though, and a couple of changes had recently taken place in the house that had once been hers exclusively. A poodle had joined the family (this was Medve) earlier and had just produced a litter of four males and seven females. This had divided Jeannie's power and popularity by twelve, and it had disheartened her. There can be no doubt but that the advent of the newcomers caused her to begin the wanderings that had taken her farther and farther away for longer and longer sojourns. Then came the final and most crushing blow, the birth of a girl baby to her owners.

Jeannie's last and futile attempt at adjustment, however sincere it may have been, and I doubt that her heart was really in it, lasted only until the baby was able to toddle around. This was, after all, a long, long time by a dog's calendar, and the fact that she was no longer the favorite in the household caused her to snap at the baby one day and bite her under the eye. This happens often, much too often, when an infant takes precedence over an old-established pet. It is a safe and highly recommended rule to follow

Thurber's Dogs

Thurber's Law in such a situation: Never bring the baby to the dog, always bring the dog to the baby.

Getting rid of a dog is not easy for any owner, but it becomes absolutely necessary if the dog turns on a child, for its hostility can never be dependably overcome. We gave Jeannie to a man and his wife who had no children and who loved dogs. They were generous with food and candy, and the new home was a paradise for a free-loader. In 1935, at the age of nine, Jeannie died, full of years and, I have no doubt, chocolates. We got a very nice letter from the people with whom she had spent her declining days. I doubt that she would have recognized us if we had called on her, or, if she had, that she would have spoken civilly to us. In a way, I suppose, you can't blame her, and I don't.

CHAPTER SIXTEEN

Blaze in the Sky

(The Curious History of a Four Weeks' Wonder)

O N JANUARY 17, 1945, an eighteen-year-old sailor, Seaman 1st Class Leon LeRoy, walked into the headquarters of the Red Cross in the little town of Antioch, California, with two problems and a grievance. He was well known in Antioch, because his father, the late Al LeRoy, had once been Chief of Police there. The young sailor's problems were routine problems, familiar to Red Cross ears anywhere: he had lost his leave papers, and he was a long way from his ship, with his furlough time running out. He wanted the Red Cross to trace his papers and to expedite his return to his post. The grievance of Leon LeRoy, however, was not so easy to classify and file. It was, indeed, a unique grievance and it smelled of news. Later in the day, Seaman LeRoy found himself repeating his story, from the beginning, to reporters.

On January 4, LeRoy said, he had come into New York harbor aboard a navy tanker on which he served as gunner. When he went ashore, he learned of the death of his father in Antioch a month before, and he applied for and received an emergency leave to visit his mother. He was put aboard a west-bound cargo plane of the Army Transport Command, at Newark. When the plane landed at Dayton, Ohio, a large wooden crate containing a bull mastiff, weighing between a hundred and ten and a hundred and thirty pounds, was put aboard. The crate took up the space of three seats. The dog's papers, which were handed to the flight engineer, included an A travel priority, and instructions on the care, exercise, and feeding of the animal. The crate was marked for delivery in Los Angeles to Faye Emerson, movie actress and wife of Lieutenant-Colonel Elliott Roosevelt.

When the plane took off for Memphis from Patterson Field, it carried not only Leon LeRoy, but two other servicemen, the time and place of whose advent my dossier of newspaper clippings does not make clear. They were Sergeant David Aks, back after thirty-one months in the Orient, and a Navy Seabee whose name and destination the newspapers did not reveal. Sergeant Aks was on his way to Riverdale, California, on emergency leave, to visit his wife, who was ill. All three men were traveling on C priorities, two notches below the A priority rating of the now celebrated Blaze, who was soaring through the air with flight credentials usually reserved for men of the highest eminence or cargo of vital and urgent importance.

It was at Memphis that the trouble began. A lieutenant of the Air Transport Command there examined Blaze's priority and then the priorities of the servicemen. He said the men would have to get off the plane to make room for three hundred pounds of B-priority freight that had piled up at the Memphis field. Blaze outranked the cargo, but the cargo outranked the servicemen. They got off the plane or, as ATC parlance has it, they were bumped off. The Seabee at this point disappears from our story forever, and we lose sight of Sergeant Aks for a time while we follow the misadventures of Leon LeRoy.

The young sailor went out into the highway and began thumbing rides. He hitchhiked his way slowly to Dallas, bemoaning the dwindling hours of his leave, and cursing, no doubt, all mastiffs and all colonels. Somewhere along the tedious route he lost his leave papers, and when he got to Dallas, the M.P.s picked him up and held him for two days. As soon as he was released, he went to the ATC in Dallas and managed at last to get on another plane headed for California.

Thurber's Dogs

When LeRoy had finished his story to the reporters, the press services went into action. Here was a news editor's dream story. It involved a dog, servicemen, a movie actress, and the Roosevelts. It smacked of arrogant goings-on in high places. There was a great shouting and scurrying and telephoning and telegraphing. Someone got hold of Sergeant Aks in Riverdale, and he corroborated the sailor's story. Mrs. Al LeRoy, Leon's mother, was worried. She told reporters she was afraid the Navy might discipline her son because of the publicity he had started.

In Granite City, Illinois, Mrs. Ola Vee Nix added to the complicated situation a new figure, Maurice Nix, Carpenter's Mate 2nd Class, U.S.N. His wife said that Nix, who had been home on emergency leave because his whole family was sick, could not get on a plane in Dallas, Texas, to return to his station because a huge mastiff had a higher travel priority. Nix had to borrow ninety-eight dollars from the Dallas Red Cross, with which he bought transportation to San Francisco on a commercial plane.

Reporters now began knocking on high official doors in Washington, demanding to know who had requested the high priority for Blaze and what official had assigned it to the dog. Secretary of War Stimson said that there had been a mistake somewhere down the line. General Harold L. George, commander of the ATC, admitted that somebody had committed an error of judgment. Presidential Secretary Stephen T. Early declared that there had been a regrettable combination of mistakes. One reporter, probing for the name of the ATC officer who had granted the priority, asked if anybody would be punished. "If you mean Sailor LeRoy," Early said, "certainly not." "No, that boy's safe all right," bawled another newsman. In Antioch a Navy representative told LeRoy that he would be given a five days' extension of leave and promised him a ride back to his tanker in a plane of the Navy Transport Command. Mrs. Al LeRoy breathed easier.

Mrs. Eleanor Roosevelt, cornered in Washington, said she did not believe any plane dispatcher would be stupid enough to put a serviceman off a plane in favor of a dog. Reporters closed in on Faye Emerson at Albuquerque when a train carrying her to Chicago stopped there. The colonel's wife said she did not believe the dog had a travel priority, and suggested that the story be carefully checked. The first she knew of Blaze's transcontinental trip, she said, was when he was delivered to her in Los Angeles by an Army major in a truck. For the first time a waiting world learned something about the bull mastiff's background. Colonel Roosevelt's wife explained that her husband wanted to breed mastiffs and that he had bought four of them in England. One had been delivered to her some months before, without any tumult or bumping, two others were still in London, and Blaze—well, the whole planet knew the whereabouts of Blaze.

In London, reporters could not find Colonel Roosevelt, but one of his aides said Elliott had left the dog with his family in Washington some time before and had asked that it be sent to his wife in Los Angeles in case any empty bomber or something was making a flight to the Coast. A War Department official, who didn't want his name used, mumbled something about comparative priorities, freight-displacement schedules, and the precedence of cargo over passengers on cargo planes. All this the New York *Herald Tribune* branded as "hilariously unsatisfactory" in an editorial which began, "We would not go so far as to say that the story of Elliott Roosevelt's dog has blanketed the news of the great Russian offensive, but we venture to guess that as a subject of discussion from coast to coast it is a strong rival," and which ended, "But let us halt before breaking into tears—unless we shed them for a family some of whose members have never learned the first rule of royalty, which is *noblesse oblige.*" The *Tribune*'s stand was supported by dozens of indignant letters in its correspondence columns.

At this juncture there was a sputtering from congressmen here and there. Representative George P. Miller of California wrote a letter to Secretary Stimson demanding a full report on what he called a

deplorable incident, and Representative Clare E.
Hoffman of Michigan brought the matter formally to
the attention of the Lower House in an impassioned
speech. He asked his colleagues what the boys in the
Pacific would think if they found out that three of
their buddies had been bumped off a plane to make
room for a dog. At this same moment, reporters were
presenting a list of typed questions to Major General
Alexander D. Surles, head of the War Department's
Bureau of Public Relations. The newspapermen
wanted the name of the culprit who had established
the A priority, and they demanded to know what
action was going to be taken to punish the fellow.
Stephen Early said he would not put the finger on
anybody, but the affair had gone too far to be dropped
so easily. The public and the press had found something pretty special to kick around, and they kicked
it around in that peculiar American way, which en-
compasses everything from elaborate gags to solemn
senatorial investigation. Everybody picked up his
phone, or got out his typewriter, or stood up and had
his say.

In Detroit, a lawyer named Herbert Denis announced that he, too, had intended to breed mastiffs,
but that the U.S. Bureau of Animal Husbandry had
refused to let him bring a male mastiff into the country three years before. The Bureau of Animal Husbandry retorted that it had no record of such a case

and did not believe Mr. Denis' dog had been refused admittance to the United States. In Granite City, Illinois, the local carpenters' union voted to refund to the Dallas Red Cross the ninety-eight dollars it had lent to Carpenter's Mate Maurice Nix. In Dallas, thirty members of that city's famous Bonehead Club tried in vain to get one of the local air lines to send to President Roosevelt, by plane, a large sad-eyed Saint Bernard wearing an opera hat. The club members then voted to send the two hundred and sixty dogs in the Dallas pound about the country in airplanes, and passed a resolution changing Groundhog Day to Grounddog Day. On this day, February 2, all dogs would be grounded so that people would get a chance to fly.

Senator Styles Bridges, Republican, of New Hampshire, hearkening to the clamor of the papers and the people, recommended a senatorial investigation of the high courtesies extended to a foreign-born mastiff. Senator Elbert D. Thomas, chairman of the Senate Military Affairs Committee, agreed with Senator Bridges and appointed a subcommittee to probe into the origin of the high priority. At this crucial and impressive moment a perfectly lovely thing happened. While journalists clucked and gloated and rubbed their hands together in fine excitement, it was revealed that the War Department had recommended seventy-seven colonels for promotion to the rank of brigadier general, and that President Roosevelt, coolly oblivious of the mastiff scandal, had sent the list of names to the Senate for its approval in spite of the fact that Elliott Roosevelt was one of the seventy-seven. "Why do they have to pick *this* time for it?" wailed Senator Albert B. ("Happy") Chandler, of Kentucky. Eyebrows lifted and tongues wagged in corridors and living rooms all over the country. A little man in a Washington restaurant observed to a tableful of total strangers that he had never heard of a colonel in all his life that he had any use for. A woman in Ohio wrote to her favorite afternoon daily crying, "Do you mean to say, for God sakes, that any Roosevelt can't just make himself a general if he wants to?"

The *Herald Tribune* added another man to the imposing battery of editorial writers it had assigned exclusively to the Blaze story. This new man had volunteered to tie up the Blaze episode with all the other tactless and arrogant mistakes of the Roosevelt regime. He wrote in part, "It will seem to a great many besides these senators that the President might have omitted his son's name from the list until he had been cleared, if that is in the cards, of responsibility for his dog's privileges. But Mr. Roosevelt's tact appears to have suffered an eclipse since his fourth inauguration. His letter to Secretary Jones asking him to make way for Mr. Wallace is a conspicuous case in point. His appointment of Aubrey Williams to head the Rural Electrification Administration is another. And now, on their heels, comes this climacteric challenge to congressional and public indignation. On top of all this can anyone be sure that he hasn't a commission in store for Blaze?"

Other newspapers followed the *Herald Tribune*'s lead, and a nasty rumble arose throughout the land. Many mothers, churchmen, and other right-thinking citizens began to fear that there would be rioting in the streets and that mastiffs and colonels would be strung up on lampposts from Tallahassee to Tacoma and from Dallas to Danbury.

It was, of all people, the United States senators, including the Republicans, who got off the first wisecracks, thus lessening the dangerous and rapidly mounting tension. "How in blazes," said Senator Bridges, "was Blaze to know he had a preferred claim? Blaze likely is an innocent victim of a poorly regulated priority system. He probably wasn't conscious of his position, except that it was comfortable and he did not care to leave the plane." Another senator who would not, understandably enough, allow his name to be used, said, "Way I look at it, the Army Transport Command is putting on a lot of dog." And he went from room to room of the Senate Office Building, repeating the gag and guffawing.

Now that the warm light of humor had begun to

play about the celebrated case, things began to fall into a proper perspective. The senators perceived that Colonel Roosevelt's connection with the notorious flight, whatever that connection may have been, had precisely nothing whatever to do with his merits as a soldier and his right to promotion. The anti-administration press continued to squawk loudly, but nobody any longer paid much attention. The affair had dragged along for almost a month, and the volatile American mind was turning to other interests.

The whole business was cleared up, once and forever, on February 10, when General George submitted a 900-word report to the subcommittee of the Senate Military Affairs Committee, in which the general placed all blame for the "inexcusable incident" on the Army's Air Transport Command. While the nation held its breath, General George pointed a shame-on-you finger at the true culprit, the official for whose blood some of the press and a part of the populace had panted since January 17. The man who had established the high priority for Blaze was Colonel Ray W. Ireland, assistant chief of staff for priorities and traffic, headquarters Air Transport Command. Colonel Ireland said that he had established the priority just as a favor. The Roosevelt family was completely absolved of any responsibility in the matter. Mrs. John Boettiger had called up the ATC from the White House about shipping Blaze to the

Coast, but she had not asked for a priority of any kind. Blaze, it turned out, had been flown from London to Washington in three different army planes, but in making the long journey he had displaced no servicemen and had broken no War Department regulation. The ATC was instructed, however, not to transport dogs, cats, mice, penguins, goldfish, or any other kind of animal life in army planes ever again.

General George's report was all right as far as it went, but it left regulation of priorities and the freight-passenger differential still pretty cloudy in the American lay mind. One of my friends, brooding over the confusing case of the bull mastiff, has suggested a card game to be called "Bumpo." If in the rapid give-and-take of cards in this game you are the first to fill your hand with seven A-priority dogs, you jump to your feet, cry "Bumpo!" and are permitted to throw your opponent or opponents out of the house.

Colonel Roosevelt and the other colonels whose promotions had been held up for nearly two weeks were made brigadier generals. In Antioch it was announced that Seaman LeRoy was going to marry a lovely girl named Barbara Warren. Thus the remarkable case of Blaze ended in a flurry of hand-shaking and congratulations all around.

A few weeks before Christmas, 1945, Blaze came to an ignoble end. He was visiting Fala, the late President Roosevelt's famous Scotty, at Hyde Park, which

Blaze in the Sky

Fala apparently decided was not big enough for two famous Roosevelt dogs. There was a brief but terrible fight one day and Fala, whose opponent outweighed him by at least 100 pounds, got the worst of it. He was taken to the hospital and Blaze was ordered destroyed. There was no uproar in the press or pulpit, and no Congressional investigation. For once the Roosevelts—men, women, and dogs—were allowed to settle a family matter privately.

Let us consign the short, unhappy life of Blaze to the silent files of time.

A PORTFOLIO

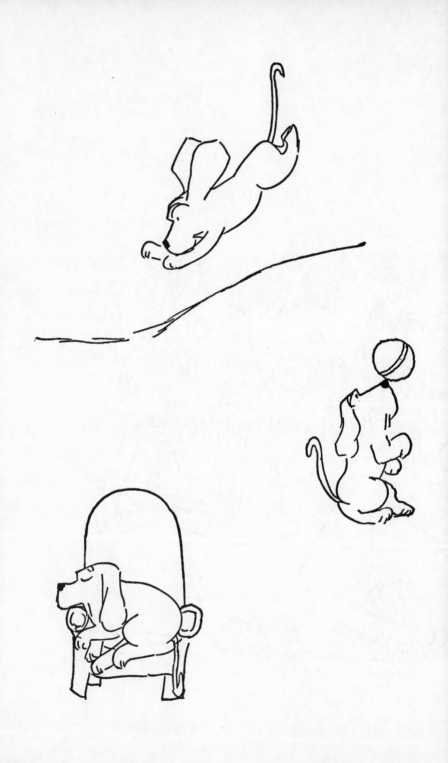

Dogs in the blizzard

Out of the storm

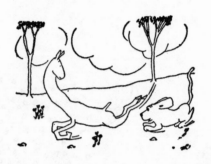

CHAPTER SEVENTEEN

The Monroes
Find a Terminal

S HORTLY AFTER NINE O'CLOCK little Mr. Monroe, who was comfortably fixed in a deep chair, under a lamp, looked up apprehensively over his book. "Where are we going?" he demanded, suspiciously.

"The French poodle gets in from Chicago tonight at nine-thirty," said his wife. "I didn't tell you before because I knew it would spoil your dinner, but it won't be anything, dear. We simply go over and pick up the puppy at the terminal so it won't have to stay all night in the crate. The shipper's letter gives all the directions." She took a letter from her handbag and gave it to her husband. Mr. Monroe, after a profound study, read one sentence aloud, slowly, "Go to

197

the West Terminal on Sixteenth Street and ask for Messenger Car of New York Central train 608, which gets in about nine-thirty."

"It's only a step . . ." Mrs. Monroe said soothingly. (The Monroes lived, at the time, in the East Sixties.)

"It's just one of those letters that never work out," said John Monroe, wisely. "We'll get away over on Sixteenth Street and we'll see a lot of big, dark, locked buildings lighted by dismal street lamps. I'll ask a man where the West Terminal is and he won't know. You can't go directly to a terminal and get a dog. I've lived long enough to know that."

"You're just trying to be ironical," said his wife. "You always make everything so hard."

"All right, all right," said Mr. Monroe, "but you'll see." He dragged out of his chair with a hard smile, got his hat and coat, and they went out and hailed a taxi.

"West Terminal," said Mrs. Monroe to the driver firmly.

"What west terminal?" asked the driver. It came out after a long talk in which Mr. Monroe, with a triumphant grin, took no part, that the taximan did not know of any west terminal where there might be a dog. Mrs. Monroe ordered him to go to Sixteenth Street and proceed slowly west, which, in the end, he did, sharing Mr. Monroe's high skepticism. The

The Monroes Find a Terminal

street was ill lighted, noisy with children. The farther
west the Monroes went, the bigger, darker, and more
firmly locked the buildings were. They passed the
M. M. Cohen Co., Paper & Twine, the Ajax Examining and Shrinking Corporation, Ozaman Club No.
2, and a copper-riveting works. Nothing looked like a
freight terminal. At the corner of Tenth Avenue,
Mrs. Monroe commanded the driver to stop near the
biggest and darkest building.

"I think this is it," she said, cheerily. Her husband
roused himself and peered out.

"National Biscuit Company," he said. "Animal
crackers. No dogs." He leaned back and smiled the
smile his wife most detested. He began to hum
slightly. The driver looked around.

"You might get out and ask somebody," said Mrs.
Monroe to her husband. This Mr. Monroe, with
strange mutterings, did. He stopped a man, conversed
briefly, and returned to the taxi.

"He says a fellow named Joe has an express office
on this street and does piano hauling," said Mr. Monroe, grimly. The chauffeur drove on. Just around the
corner in Eleventh Avenue, a hopeful-looking struc-
ture loomed up. Mr. Monroe looked out.

"The Economy Wiping Materials Company," he
said.

"I can read," said his wife, shortly. After a moment

she gave a little cry. "Look, John," she said, "there it
is!" She pointed at some freight cars in a small yard
across the avenue. A light glowed in a shack marked
"N. Y. C. R. R." They got out of the cab and stumbled
across the street. A short, gray, deaf man with silver-
rimmed spectacles answered their knock at the door
of the shack. He failed from the first to get it quite
clear in his mind what was wanted, but he got enough
to affirm definitely that there was no poodle in the
yards there.

"Where do you think the dog would be?" Mrs.
Monroe asked him.

"Lady," he said, "I don't know," and disappeared.

Mrs. Monroe was for going into the yards and
knocking on freight cars. "He might bark," she explained.

Mr. Monroe led her back to the taxi. "You can't get
a dog from a terminal by force," he said, sternly.
"We'll go back home and think this thing out. First
of all, is it coming freight or express—do you know
that?" He had assumed his protective, man-of-the-
world attitude.

"The express company is shipping it by freight,"
said his wife, somewhat subdued by the experiences
of the evening.

"They don't do that," said Mr. Monroe. "The two
things are separate." His tone, however, carried little

conviction. "Probably express," he added. "I think it's only furniture that comes freighted."

"I don't suppose," said Mrs. Monroe, "they've given the poor doggy any water."

"The dog has water; we'll get the dog," said her husband with his best executive air.

"I don't know," his wife said doubtfully. "They step on their bowls." They drove home in silence.

Back at the apartment, he asked for the phone book, and Mrs. Monroe finally found it on Mr. Monroe's bed. "Now," he said, "look up under New York Central." She did and began to read off, " 'General and Exec——' "

"Go on," said Mr. Monroe.

" 'Freight stations,' " continued his wife, " 'Pier 34 ER ft Rutgers slip, St. John Pk Laight & Varick ——' "

"Give me the book," said Mr. Monroe importantly. He took it, flipped over a few pages, frowned, and began to look around nervously.

"Under your chair," said his wife. He reached under his chair and found his tobacco pouch. "Now look under American Railway Express," pursued his wife. Mr. Monroe did this, after filling his pipe.

"Here we are," he said, " 'American Railway Express: Tracing department, Claim department, On Hand department'—ah, that's probably it—'438

Thurber's Dogs

West Fifty-fifth.' When things are received they are considered on hand and ——"

"It couldn't be that," interrupted his wife. "That's where they have dogs for a week or more. Let me have the book." She went over and took it. Carefully and calmly she studied the listings. "Here!" she said, " 'Terminals: Tenth Avenue and Thirty-third, Lexington and Forty-ninth.' Now Lexington is east and the other west—it must be Tenth Avenue and Thirty-third. I'll call that number."

"No use," said her husband, pityingly. He yawned and began to remove his shoes. "The shipper couldn't have been that far off—from Sixteenth to Thirty-third Street. If you phone there, a guy will answer in a German accent and deny everything. Wait till morning and I'll call up a ——"

But Mrs. Monroe was already on the phone. Suddenly she was talking, animatedly. "Yes, 608. A little black dog. It is? Oh, you did? Well, that's fine! We'll be right up!" She hung up the receiver. "It's there!" she cried. "The man said he had seen the puppy—the car was just brought in up there. Hurry, let's go right up and get it! It must be thirsty."

Mr. Monroe did not hurry. He put his shoes back on slowly, smiling strangely, like a diplomat at a conference.

"You see, my dear," he began, as they started out again, "you have to go at these things carefully and

The Monroes Find a Terminal

calmly and figure out logically where a dog, shipped from Chicago, would most naturally ——" His wife smiled, even more strangely than he had, and kissed him.

"My great big wonderful husband," she said. "He thinks of everything."

CHAPTER EIGHTEEN

And So to Medve

DOG MAY BE MAN'S BEST FRIEND, but Man is often Dog's severest critic, in spite of his historic protestations of affection and admiration. He calls an unattractive girl a dog, he talks acidly of dogs in the manger, he describes a hard way of life as a dog's life, he observes, cloudily, that this misfortune or that shouldn't happen to a dog, as if most slings and arrows should, and he describes anybody he can't stand as a dirty dog. He notoriously takes the names of the female dog and her male offspring in vain, to denounce blackly members of his own race. In all this disdain and contempt there is a curious streak of envy, akin to what the psychiatrists know as sibling jealousy. Man is troubled by what might be called the Dog Wish, a strange and involved compulsion to be as happy and carefree as a dog, and I hope that some

Thurber's Dogs

worthy psychiatrist will do a monograph on it one of these days. Even the Romans of two thousand years ago displayed the peculiar human ambivalence about the dog. There are evidences, in history and literature, of the Romans' fondness for the dog, and my invaluable Cassell's Latin Dictionary reveals proof of their hostility. Among the meanings of *canis* were these: a malicious, spiteful person; a parasite, a hanger-on. The worst throw in dice was also known to the Romans as a dog. Caesar may have been afraid he would throw a dog that day he crossed the Rubicon.

Tracing aspersions on the dog in literature and in

And So to Medve

common everyday speech is a task for some stronger authority than I, such as the Oxford English Dictionary, but there are a few calumnies that I might glance at here, in passing. I remember when "Don't be an Airedale all your life" was a common expression in the Middle West, and a man I knew in Zanesville thirty years ago used the expression a dozen times a day. Shakespeare takes many cracks at Dog from "I would rather be a dog and baying the moon than such a Roman" to "Turn, hellhound!" which Macduff hurls at the bloody Macbeth to start their fifth-act duel with broadswords. The Bard, knowing full well that it is men who are solely responsible for wars, nevertheless wrote "Cry havoc, and let loose the dogs of war!" But it is not only in the classics that the much-maligned hound has been attacked. A craven pugilist is known to boxing fans as a hound. And I have always resented the words Whittier put in Stonewall Jackson's mouth: "Who touches a hair on yon gray head dies like a dog!" Here it is implied that any soldier who took a free shot at Barbara Frietchie would be shot, and shooting is rarely the end of a dog. There are a score of birds and animals which could more aptly have been substituted for the dog and I suggest "Who touches a hair on yon gray head dies like a duck!" But, alas, these ancient libels are past erasing, and Dog will simply have to go on enduring them as patiently as he can.

Thurber's Dogs

Stanley Walker, in the old debate of ours that fell so far below the Scopes trial in public interest, condemned the gush that has been written about dogs, as if they and not the female of our own species were the principal object of the sentimental output of men. The truth is that both Dog and Woman have received through the ages undeserved abuse and fulsome praise in about equal measure. But when it comes to the highest praise, for woodwinds, strings, and brasses, Man's favorite theme is the male human being. He describes Woman as a ministering angel, but of himself he cries, "How like a god!"

I wrote somewhere a long time ago that I am not a "dog-lover," that to me a dog-lover is a dog in love with another dog, and I went on to say that liking or disliking varied, in my case, with the individual dog as with the individual person. Comparing the two breeds as such takes a critic onto sensitive ground, where the climate is changeable and the air is stuffy. A discussion of the relative merits of the ape and the wolf would interest me more than a debate about men and canines. In such a debate the dog could not take part, and when Man began to talk loosely about his Best Friend, or himself, I would reach for my hat and find my way to a neighborhood bar.

Most writers on dogs insist on viewing the animal in a human light, as they insist on teaching it tricks that amuse only humans, and the things people admire

most in a dog are their own virtues, strangely magnified and transfigured. A man, to hear him tell it,
thinks that lying for several days and nights on a grave
is the highest possible expression of loyalty, faithful-
ness, and devotion, and the finest demonstration of
grief. Albert Payson Terhune labored to lift the collie
not only above all other dogs in sensitivity and aware-
ness, but seemed to have considered its standards of
judgment often superior to those of the human being.
He actually believed that his collies stalked out of the
room in a show of moral disapproval when whisky
was poured into glasses, and never considered the
strong probability that the dogs couldn't stand the
fumes of alcohol in their sensitive and aware nostrils,
and just walked away. When my mother used to say
that Muggs, our mordant Airedale, could read a man
like a book, she always implied that the dog was con-
versant with the fellow's weaknesses of character.
After Muggs had read a man like a book he always
growled at him or made his fierce biting leap. In other
words, Muggs was a moralist and a reformer, out to
punish the weakling and the sinner.

Mother-love, as we call it, the strongest instinct in
the female of any species, has always been the most
flexible implement in the hands of the sentimentalist.
The Scotch collies and the border collies that take
part every year in the sheep-dog trials in Scotland are
hard-working, well-trained, shrewd sheep dogs whose

arduous careers have turned them into realists. I have always believed that human fancy adorned one of my favorite Mother-love legends about these collies. The tale tells that a female that had gone out to bark the cattle home was whelped of half a dozen pups, and promptly tucked five of them under a log, picked up the sixth by the scruff of its neck, and came home behind the cows as always, except for the odd, muffled sound of her bark. She then, of course, led her master back to the log. He had sense enough to take a basket, and the pups were brought home in that. My own conviction, after years of meditation about it, is that the collie left all six pups under the log, brought the cows home, and then led her master to where she had hidden the litter. If you have just delivered six pups, you don't have to carry one of them in your mouth to convince a dog-owner, even a male dog-owner, that a series of blessed events has taken place.

A long time ago, I drove a secondhand Ford sedan up to the Scottish field trials one summer's day. The competition brings together the most experienced sheep dogs of the British Isles. It was won that year, for the second straight time, by an old professional yellow-and-white female with only one eye (maybe she had hidden her puppies under somebody else's log and got a poke in the eye for her intrusion). These dogs have been as carefully educated as bloodhounds or police dogs, and the old-timers go out, bring back six sheep from a distant hill, and put them through all sorts of difficult maneuvers. Each dog is aided only by the whistle signals of his master. Speed and accuracy and smartness of performance count in these sheep-dog trials. The day I was there, a young male collie, a novice in sheep-herding, made his debut, went completely to pieces when his sheep refused to enter a small pen at his bidding, promptly sat down on his haunches, and howled to high heaven. He was disqualified but was cheered by the gallery as his master led him away. But let us get back to America.

One day I heard an anthropologist say that a dog gets whatever conscience it has from its master. The eminent scientist almost stumbled into a familiar trap when he began beating the bushes of this tricky terrain: the assumption that the whole pattern of a dog's behavior, even its own familiar rituals and duties, have to be inculcated in the beast by the Great God Man. Anybody who has observed the behavior of a canine bitch and her litter, from whelping to weaning, knows that this particular piece of human pretension is nonsense. Dogs may have only a sensory, and not a historical, memory, they may have to depend on instinct instead of precept, and their reasoning may lack the advantages of accumulated knowledge, but a female dog knows more about raising her own pups (I except only Jeannie) than any man or woman could

teach her. A bitch's discipline is her own, and it lacks
the pride, idealism, and dreams of the human female,
but it works beautifully and with an admirable economy of effort.

This brings us to Medve (Hungarian for "bear"),
my first black standard French poodle, whose posture
of repose and thoughtful eyes gave her the appearance of a reflective intellectual, absorbed by the mysterious clockwork ticking behind the outward show
of mundane phenomena. Her expression, in these moments of meditation, seemed to be one of compassion,
as against the deep contemplative look of the bloodhound, whose sadness, more apparent than real, appears to have grown out of a long consideration of
Man's queer habit of becoming lost, stolen, wounded,
or crooked. We read most of these thoughts into dogs,
as we invent other human qualities for them, but
anybody who has known dogs well, and studied them
fairly, over a period of fifty years, realizes, without
being able to prove it, that not all of their peculiar
abilities are invented by human romantics. Medve
was a dog who could entertain herself and do without
human companionship for long hours on end. She
liked to retrieve the apples she found in season under
the russet tree, but she had just as much fun throwing
an apple herself and chasing it as letting me in on the
game. She would pull her head far around to the left,
give the apple a quick, hard toss, downhill always, and

then chase it and bring it back. She liked to go out into the woods by herself, but what solitary games she may have played there I never found out.

Medve was a professional show dog, who once went Best of Breed at the Westminster Show, but she hated public appearances and was happiest living in the country, where she raised two litters of eleven pups each, seven females and four males both times. She was a professional mother, too. One of the pups of the second litter was continually complaining, in the days immediately following its weaning, that it was sick and had to have milk. Medve would patiently examine the pup with practiced expertness, and, satisfied that it was pretending, push it rudely away with her muzzle. Once, when it became unusually obstreperous, she sent it tumbling over and over. It staggered to its feet, put on a show of limping worthy of a ham actor, and announced, in a kind of squeal I had never heard before, that it had been mortally wounded. Medve went over and picked it up and gave it the careful examination that a squirrel gives a nut, turning it over and over carefully. Satisfied, at last, that it wasn't even hurt, let alone dying, she gave it another, but gentler, shove, and stalked out of its presence and into the house.

She could tell, from thirty yards away, the quality and meaning of her puppies' whimpers, screams, squeals, and protests. When an outcry of any kind began, she would lift her head and listen intently. I never learned to tell the difference between one puppy cry and another, but she knew them all. Often she would saunter out to where the puppies were kept, taking her time; once in a while she would run to them swiftly, like a mother who has got an urgent telephone call, but mostly she would just sigh, put her head on her paws, and go to sleep. She managed the tedium of motherhood with the special grace and dignity of her breed. Scotch Jeannie, on the other hand, went around wearing a martyred look when she had pups to care for, as if she had invented parturition and wished she could turn it off, like a faucet. She responded to every call from the puppy basket with a frown of desperation, and I don't believe she could tell a yip from a yelp, or a yap from a yowl. She was a setup for the deceitful tactics of her offspring (she didn't even know how to snap an umbilical cord, and usually asked for human help).

Medve, both times, had more puppies than there was room for at table, as one lady writer has put the not uncommon problem, and she didn't know how to take care of this nutritional situation, as smart as she was. I have collected a dozen romantic newspaper clippings on this subject, the most recent this year about a Great Dane bitch who had fourteen pups and not enough dugs to accommodate them. This animal, according to solemn report, developed a command of

A litter of perfectly healthy puppies raised on fried pancakes.

mathematics and divided the pups into two groups of seven each, so that there were two separate shifts, or servings. If one of the lustier youngsters came back for a second helping, it seems that he was promptly muzzled away. My own experience with dogs has invariably demonstrated the dietary survival of the strongest, and human control is necessary if the weaker pups are not to be undernourished. If Medve couldn't deal with this predicament, then no other dog could. She never rolled on any of her twenty-two pups and crushed them, but this clumsy disaster is common in the case of Great Danes, bloodhounds, and other females of the larger varieties, as it is with tigresses and lionesses in the jungle. There is no sagacious selectivity in it, either, just pure accident. Medve's conscience, in answering or ignoring the commands of her young, was her inherited own, and none of my business, and probably beyond the comprehension of even the most celebrated anthropologists.

In the case of one of her whelpings, the father of the litter kept hanging around, I forget just why, and, in the manner of the male tiger, he began giving the pups boxing lessons when he thought they were old enough to enjoy rough and tumble. If he got too rough and tumbled one of the pups too far, so that it squeaked, Medve would go for him, with low head and low growl, and nip him on the shoulder and drive him away. The male tiger, incidentally, slips off by himself into the jungle when the female is about to produce cubs, and doesn't return from the bars and the night clubs until the cubs are fairly well grown, thus avoiding sleepless nights, and annoyance in general. Mother-love, in beasts and birds, can't always be observed carefully, because of innate animal secrecy, but—to revisit an old Ohio highway for a moment— I once encountered a mother quail leading her young across the road in single file. She diverted my attention from them by pretending to have a broken wing, and flopped around almost at my feet, in an exhibition of bravura acting something like that of the late Lionel Barrymore as Rasputin. When the small birds had disappeared into the deep grass, she flew calmly away and joined them. The domesticated dog, to be sure, is accustomed to human interference with its young, and will usually tolerate it patiently. Jeannie was a snapper, though—she once broke the neck of a Siamese cat that approached her puppy basket—and I am glad that it was Medve's litter and not Jeannie's which my two-year-old daughter discovered one day in the barn, and began playing with. Jeannie was as inept in a barn with her young as she was in a shoe closet, and once when she lost a pup under a floor board she trotted outside and began frantically digging, with one paw, at the base of the stone foundation. I estimated that she would have reached the skeleton of her pup, by that terrier method, in approximately fourteen weeks. (The same thing happened to Tessa, another Scotty of mine, as I have reported somewhere earlier.) The poodle had sense enough to pry up the floor board in such an emergency, or to ask for help from somebody with muscle and fingers.

A strange phenomenon of family feud, which I was never able to figure out, occurred in the bringing up of Medve's first litter. One of the pups, to me as handsome and genial as any of the others, became an outcast, and its ten siblings continually abused it. In the early weeks Medve always took its part and chastised the attackers, but after they were all weaned she gave the problem no further thought, and I had to drag the culprits away from their victim. The human mother, as I have said before and now say again, devotes her entire life to her young and to her young's young, a life of continual concern and anguish, full of local and long-distance telephone calls, letters and telegrams, restless nights and worried days, but Medve, like all of her ilk, refused to be bothered after the first few months. She once allowed six of her pups, long past the weaning stage, to take a portable victrola apart, scatter records all over the place, and chew off, with active and eager teeth, one leg of an upright ping-pong table, causing a landslide of paddles and balls, books, ash trays, and magazines. As long as the grown pups didn't pester Medve, their life was their own, but if she was badgered, she had a unique way of putting the dog in its place, jumping over it gracefully, and giving it a good cuff on the head with one of her hind paws.

Medve's profound dislike of show business caused her to develop a kind of Freudian car-sickness, because riding in a car had so often meant a trip to a dog show, as did the long and irritating process of trimming. She was made to wear a red rubber bib, tied around her neck, and a newspaper was always placed on the floor of the car. She threw up on it like a lady, leaning far down, looking as apologetic as she looked sick. At one of the last dog shows in which she was entered with two or three of her best male pups, she was reluctant to get up on the bench assigned to her and her family, and so I got up on it myself, on all fours, to entice her to follow. She was surprised and amused, but not interested, and this was also true of my wife, who kept walking past the bench, saying, out of the corner of her mouth, "Get off that bench, for the love of heaven!" She finally got me off, and the dogs on. The dogs all thought it had been a wonderful interlude, except Medve, who, I am sure, had had a momentary high hope that I was going to take her place in the show.

Medve lived to be fourteen, and after she died I wrote a piece about her called "Memorial" for the newspaper *PM,* which died not long afterward. Of the three of us, I am now the only one left. The brief eulogy, written so soon after my bereavement, has a sunset touch here and there, but I have decided not to let my older and colder hand and mind blur its somewhat dramatic feeling. I know now, and knew then, that no dog is fond of dying, but I have never had a dog that showed a human, jittery fear of death, either. Death, to a dog, is the final unavoidable compulsion, the last ineluctable scent on a fearsome trail, but they like to face it alone, going out into the woods, among the leaves, if there are any leaves when their time comes, enduring without sentimental human distraction the Last Loneliness, which they are wise enough to know cannot be shared by anyone. If your dog has to go, he has to go, and it is better to let him go alone. Dogs have little sense of time and they are not comforted by tearful good-bys, only by cheerful greetings. Here, then, with a trace of repetition that I trust will be forgiven, is the piece from *PM*.

CHAPTER NINETEEN

Memorial

S HE CAME ALL THE WAY from Illinois by train in a big wooden crate many years ago, a frightened black poodle, not yet a year old. She felt terrible in body and worse in mind. These contraptions that men put on wheels, in contravention of that law of nature which holds that the feet must come in contact with the ground in traveling, dismayed her. She was never able to ride a thousand yards in an automobile without getting sick at her stomach, but she was always apologetic about this frailty, never, as she might well have been, reproachful.

She tried patiently at all times to understand Man's way of life: the rolling of his wheels, the raising of his voice, the ringing of his bells; his way of searching out with lights the dark protecting corners of the night; his habit of building his beds inside walls, high above the nurturing earth. She refused, with all courtesy, to accept his silly notion that it is better to bear puppies in a place made of machined wood and clean blue cloth than in the dark and warm dirt beneath the oak flooring of the barn.

The poodle was hand in glove with natural phenomena. She raised two litters of puppies, taking them in her stride, the way she took the lightning and the snow. One of these litters, which arrived ahead of schedule, was discovered under the barn floor by a little girl of two. The child gaily displayed on her right forearm the almost invisible and entirely painless marks of teeth which had gently induced her to put down the live black toys she had found and wanted to play with.

The poodle had no vices that I can think of, unless you could count her incurable appetite for the tender tips of the young asparagus in the garden and for the black raspberries when they ripened on the bushes in the orchard. Sometimes, as punishment for her depredations, she walked into bees' nests or got her long shaggy ears tangled in fence wire. She never snarled about the penalties of existence or whimpered about the trials and grotesqueries of life with Man.

She accepted gracefully the indignities of the clipping machine which, in her maiden days, periodically made a clown of her for the dog shows, in accordance with the stupid and unimaginative notion that this most sensitive and dignified of animals is at heart a buffoon. The poodle, which can look as husky as a Briard when left shaggy, is an outdoor dog and can hold its own in the field with the best of the retrievers, including the Labrador.

The poodle won a great many ribbons in her bench days, but she would have traded all her medals for a dish of asparagus. She knew it was show time when the red rubber bib was tied around her neck. That meant a ride in a car to bedlam.

Like the great Gammeyer of Tarkington's *Gentle Julia,* the poodle I knew seemed sometimes about to bridge the mysterious and conceivably narrow gap that separates instinct from reason. She could take part in your gaiety and your sorrow; she trembled to your uncertainties and lifted her head at your assurances. There were times when she seemed to come close to a pitying comprehension of the whole troubled scene and what lies behind it. If poodles, who walk so easily upon their hind legs, ever do learn the little tricks of speech and reason, I should not be surprised if they made a better job of it than Man, who would seem to be surely but not slowly slipping back to all fours.

The poodle kept her sight, her hearing, and her figure up to her quiet and dignified end. She knew that the Hand was upon her and she accepted it with a grave and unapprehensive resignation. This, her

Thurber's Dogs

dark intelligent eyes seemed to be trying to tell me, is simply the closing of full circle, this is the flower that grows out of Beginning; this—not to make it too hard for you, friend—is as natural as eating the raspberries and raising the puppies and riding into the rain.

CHAPTER TWENTY

Christabel
Part One *

PRESIDENT TRUMAN has revealed a talent for name-calling that would win the admiration of old Andy Jackson, who got shot at in battle, fought half a dozen duels, but would have blanched at the thought of insulting the United States Marines. The President's big slur, for which he so bravely and handsomely apologized later, rang the swords and helmets in the halls of Montezuma and startled the very sands on the shores of Tripoli. And then, while the nation was still buzzing indignantly, Mr. Truman suddenly whizzed his fast ball under the chin of John L. Lewis, declaring that far from making the labor leader Ambassador to Moscow, he wouldn't even appoint him dogcatcher.

* From *The Bermudian,* 1950.

225

Thurber's Dogs

Now, Mr. Lewis likes nothing better than an exchange of epithets at thirty paces, so he got out his bejeweled duelling pistols and blazed away. As so often happens in these word battles, one of his shots hit an innocent bystander, that old friend of mine, the French poodle. He charged that certain employees of the State Department were "intellectual poodle dogs." The bronze-tongued orator of the coal mines obviously sought to imply by this invidious and gratuitous crack that poodle dogs are intelligent fools.

Now I am a close friend of poodle dogs, having had a lot of them in my time, twenty-five in all, to be exact. I have never known, or even heard of, a bad poodle. Theirs is the most charming of species, including the human, and they happily lack Man's aggression, irritability, quick temper, and wild aim. They have courage, too, and they fight well and fairly when they have to fight. The poodle, moving into battle, lowers its head, attacks swiftly, and finishes the business without idle rhetoric or false innuendo. One spring my French poodle, who was nine years old at the time, killed three red squirrels in ten seconds, thus saving the lives of hundreds of songbirds, the natural prey of the red marauders. She has never attacked a gray squirrel or a friendly dog, and while she has admittedly engaged in a cold war with cats since 1942, she is too gentle, and too smart, to try to take one apart to find out what makes it purr.

Christabel: Part One

I must confess that many poodles are afraid of lightning, slamming doors, pistol shots, high winds, and things that go bump in the night, but then so am I. Some of them are high-strung and nervous, but few are neurotic, and they have sensitivity, humor, and dignity. My own poodle is a connoisseur of food one day, and a vulgar gourmand the next. She likes rare steak, frogs' legs Provençale, paté, cheese of any kind, chocolate in any form, and a horrible assortment of things she finds in the fields and woods, old and new, buried and blue. Like most human males, she regards lettuce and the other ingredients of green salads as rabbit food. How any dog who eats a soufflé with dainty and intense enjoyment can leap upon a milk-bone or the awful glop called dog candy with equal interest is beyond my understanding. Poodles hate to have their ears monkeyed with or their temperature taken, just as I do, and, like me, they are convinced that creatures who live in holes in the ground must be three times as large as they really are. They are amiable and tolerant, with a healthy prejudice against motorcyclists, tree surgeons, and skiing instructors. They are fond of the butcher, the baker, and the grocer, but hold that the visits of the laundryman and the dry cleaner make no sense and should be discouraged. They make wonderful companions, confidants, and house guests, and are amenable to argument and persuasion. My poodle and I disagree on only two subjects. She contends that my car is a Poodillac and belongs to her and not to me, and that the sound of thunder is made by a four-footed monster the size of a mountain. There is only one flaw in my poodle's honor: she has been known to steal a fried-egg sandwich from me, and then tell my wife that I gave it to her.

A lot of my friends own poodles, among them Charles Addams, the famed connoisseur of ghouls. His poodle's name is Tulip. You want to make anything out of it, Mr. Lewis?

The poodle makes an excellent gun dog and, in the annual American field trials, often wins out over the other retrievers. My own dog was not trained as a retriever and now, at the age of nine, she is convinced that chasing a ball and bringing it back is a futile form of vicious circle, leaving you in the end tired out and just where you were when you started. But she loves to play hide-and-seek, and the day always begins in my house with a foolish attempt on my part to hide from her in one of the eight upstairs rooms. When she finds me—and it usually takes her less than ten seconds —she grins from ear to ear, her eyes twinkle, and she makes the unmistakable sound of laughter. The only time I ever fooled her was one morning when I called to her and then crawled back in bed. This was against the rules of the game and she was reproachful about it and refused to shake hands with me until late in the afternoon.

The John L. Lewises have gained a distorted notion about poodles because of the unfortunate custom of trimming them in a comic way for dog shows. This deplorable habit of making clowns out of humorists was once thought to go back to the reign of a cruel and playful Roman emperor, but the breed isn't that old. Some of us have hopes that the show trim will be abandoned one day, giving the poodle a chance to establish its true identity and its real nature. In the past twenty years, poodles have become more and more popular in America and have reached the point where they can walk along a street without being jeered at. In 1929, however, a poodle of mine, shown at the Westminster show in New York, had such little opposition that she won the blue ribbon in her class after having been displayed for only two minutes. The lady who was showing her in the ring was so surprised when the judge gave her dog first prize that she burst into tears. The poodle instantly began to howl, too, in the mistaken belief that their mingled tears were meant to express disapproval of the judge, the bedlam, and the whole distressing spectacle.

The poodle is a freedom-loving dog and does not like to be confined. My present poodle once beat and bit her way through the window of a closed car.

Thurber's Dogs

Poodles can learn to be seeing-eye dogs in half the time it takes the members of any other breed, but they are rarely used for this purpose because their independent spirit rebels against the repetition of a pattern, because they hate muzzles and leashes, and because they insist on inventing rules of their own. Poodles are great believers in liberty, a thing becoming rare in our day, and they should be allowed to enjoy it.

When my poodle dies, I will bury her sorrowfully under the apple tree, and remember her bright spirit and her gentle gaiety all the years of my life.

CHAPTER TWENTY-ONE

Christabel
Part Two

MY POODLE was fourteen years old last May and she is still immensely above ground. She slips more easily than she used to on linoleum, makes strange sounds in her sleep, and sighs a great deal, but more as if she had figured something out than given it up. Her ears are not as sharp as they were, and she often barks at things that aren't there, and sleeps through things that are. Her eyes are not much better than mine, but since she can still smell her way around as well as ever, she bumps into fewer things than I do. I have heard whispers, or maybe I just imagine I heard them, that the poodle will live to see *me* laid to rest under the apple tree. When she fell a year ago on the kitchen linoleum and sprained her right shoulder,

the veterinarian gave her a couple of shots of corti-
sone, and she came bounding merrily home from the
kennels with the high heart of a schoolgirl on vacation, insisting that our clocks were two hours slow and
that it was time for dinner. Some day, long after I am
gone, the people who now stop at my front door to ask
their way to the Cathedral Pines will want to know
if they can show their grandchildren the forty-year-
old French poodle.

The poodle's kennel name was Christabel, and she
is a *caniche moyen,* or medium-sized French standard
poodle. Most people think of all poodles, standard or
miniature or toy, black or white or brown, as French,
and so did I until a few years ago when I began nosing about in dog books and dictionaries. The poodle
actually gets its name from the German word *"pud-
(d)el,"* meaning to splash in water, for these dogs,
originally German, were used to retrieve wild ducks
shot down over lakes. Legend has it that a hunting
poodle would swim around all night in a lake hunting
for a lost duck, which brings us to an ingenious explanation of the so-called Continental trim of the poodle,
familiar to everybody and ridiculous to many. It
seems that the back part of the poodle's body was
clipped to give it greater agility and speed in the
water, that the "bracelets" on the front legs and the
pompons or epaulettes near the hip bones were left

there to prevent joints from becoming stiff after a long cold patrol of the fowling waters. The tale also tells (most recently in T. H. Tracy's *The Book of the Poodle*) that the pompon on the end of the stubby tail was put there to serve as a kind of periscope by which the hunter could follow the movements of his dog in the water! The exclamation point is mine, because it is surely the front part of the swimming dog that can be most easily detected, and I am certain that before long somebody will put forward the theory that the red ribbon found in the head hair of some poodles was originally tied there to help the duck hunter locate his circling dog.

Defense counsel for the poodle has his work cut out for him, no matter who makes up the jury he addresses—canine-haters, bassett- or boxer-owners, or lapdog dowagers. The word "poodle" itself is bad enough, but the kennel names of individual members of the breed are worse: Tiddly Winks Thistledown of White Hollow, Twinkle Toes the Third, Little Chief Thunderfoot of Creepaway, and other unlikely compounds of whipped cream and frustrated mother-love, or whatever it may be that causes this sort of thing. The poodle strain caught the fancy some years ago of Park Avenue, Broadway, and Beverly Hills, and these unions have brought about such pet home names as Chi Chi, Frou Frou, Pouf Pouf, Zsa Zsa, and for God's sake don't let me go on like this. The ornamental trim of the poodle, grimly *de rigueur* in dog shows everywhere because it is said to be the best way to exhibit the dog's coat and some of its other show points, has prejudiced people against the great duck retriever for almost five hundred years. (There seems to be no valid evidence of the existence of poodles much earlier than the last half of the fifteenth century, and the tale of the antic Roman emperor who had them clipped to look like lions is, of course, apocryphal.) Whatever the truth may be, the poodle would probably have been laughed out of town and country long ago, had it not been for the sound and attractive clip known as the Dutch trim.

The poodle has been the butt of jokes, all of them pallid as far as I can find out, from Benjamin Disraeli to John L. Lewis, and this had helped to perpetuate the libel that the most sagacious of dogs is an aimless and empty-headed comic. Most apologists, in trying to defend the poodle against this calumny, succeed in making him sound foolisher and foolisher. Very few persons have successfully transcribed the comic talents of a poodle into prose, whether typed or conversational. Something vital and essential dies in the telling of a poodle story. It is like a dim recording of a bad W. C. Fields imitator. My poodle, I am glad to say, does not meet a gentleman caller at the door and take his hat and gloves, or play the piano for guests, or move chessmen about upon a board, or wear glasses and smoke a pipe, or lift the receiver off the phone, or spell out your name in alphabet blocks, or sing "Madelon," or say "Franchot Tone," or give guests their after-dinner coffee cups. She is as smart as any of her breed; indeed she has taken on a special wisdom in what some would estimate to be her seventy-fifth, others her one-hundred-and-fifth year, as human lives are measured, but she has never been trained to do card tricks, or go into dinner on a gentleman's arm, or to say "Beowulf," or even "Ralph." I once tried to get her to ring an old Bermuda carriage bell I picked up years ago, but she was disdainful of this noisy waste of time, and was even more reluctant when I tried to get her to step on the rubber bulb of a 1905 automobile horn. She doesn't like strange unnecessary sounds; she likes quiet and tranquillity.

No, my aged water-splasher has never been taught any tricks that make dinner guests and week-end visitors alert and nervous. If you open the door of your bedroom in the morning, she is not standing there with a newspaper and a glass of orange juice. Somebody once tried to show her how to carry the mail into the house, and she gaily spread the letters all over the front lawn, a lighthearted and sensible way of dealing with my correspondence, which consists largely of invitations to address the Men's Forum of Dismal Seepage, Ohio, requests for something intimate to raffle off at a church bazaar, and peremptory demands, such as: "My sister-in-law has ulcers. Please send her six drawings." The poodle will shake hands, in the gracious manner of her breed, and engage in impromptu house games and lawn games, but she will not appear suddenly at your elbow at the cocktail hour carrying a plate of hors d'oeuvres. She is a country dog, and trembles all over when she is driven in to New York, which isn't often, but the atavistic urge to hunt and swim must have gone out of her bloodline generations ago, leaving no trace. She couldn't tell a mallard or a canvasback from a Plymouth Rock hen, and gunfire appalls her. She can swim a little, but would rather wade. She has never tangled with a skunk or a porcupine, and she has the good sense to beg a woodchuck's pardon if she trespasses on its property, and go back home. When she dances on her hind legs, down near the brook, it means she has discovered a snake, but she would no more close in on one than I would wrassle a bear. She has been known to follow a frog or a toad for hours, with the expression of one who does not believe her own nose. The rabbits who share my garden produce found out years ago that they could outrun and outzigzag the poodle, and a red fox who lives nearby once trotted right past her, down the driveway and out onto the road, as big as you please. One night the old dog followed a possum up into the woods and didn't come back for two hours. It was my daughter's opinion that the possum had held the poodle for ransom, but finally decided to let her go. This is calumny of a familiar kind and the poodle is used to it. She is not a hunter or a killer, but an interested observer of the life of the lower animals, of which she does not consider herself one. She regards herself as a member of the human race and, as such, she sees no fun or profit in chasing a ball or a stick and bringing it back, time and again. A hundred terriers have made me miserable since before the First World War by laying a ball at my feet and standing there panting and gasping and drooling until I throw it. Nobody my age can throw a baseball as far as I can, because of these long years of practice. I am told that one short-haired fox terrier, for whom I threw a ball all one afternoon, never did come back when I finally wound up and let go. Goody.

In her old age, the Dowager Duchess of West Cornwall has become a touch imperious and has firmly taken her place as a co-equal in the conduct of certain household affairs, particularly those involving meals. She used to lie obediently in the living room, with her paws just over the threshold, but if you are a poodle going on seventy-five or a hundred-and-five, you waive, without consultation, the old rules of behavior. She now removes toast from my grasp if I let my hand fall below what she has established as the point of no return, and now and then she removes from my lap, with a brisk dainty gesture, my napkin, on the ground that the crumbs it has collected belong to her. If you tell her to go in and lie down when you have a dish she especially craves in front of you, she stomps her feet and communicates her flat refusal in a series of guttural sounds very much like an attempt at words. Her range of inflection and intonation, after a decade and a half with people, is remarkable, and I am now able to tell by the quality of her voice, when she is outdoors, who is approaching the house. She not only divides tradespeople into her own classifications, but she has stratified certain friends and acquaintances of ours. Every dog does this, in its minor instinctive way, but without the almost verbal criticism Christabel can bring to her welcome or her inhospitality. She is no longer very hospitable to any caller or visitor, but once a person gets inside the house, she becomes in a flash the perfect hostess, shaking hands, sniffing pockets or purses to see if they contain chocolates or something dug up out of the ground.

She realized, two or three times as quickly as a member of any other breed could have done it, that I had got so that I couldn't see her, and she gets up quietly when I enter a room where she is lying. Once, when I stumbled into her and fell sprawling, she hurriedly examined me from head to foot, with a show of great anxiety, as if she were looking for compound fractures. Christabel regards me as a comedian of sorts, and always knows when I am trying to be funny for her sake, and always smiles (there is no smile quite like a poodle's), and if the joke is a big production number, such as my opening the door to the downstairs lavatory when she asks to be let out, she gives her guttural laugh, turns her head slowly, and lets my wife in on the gag. Now and then she has disapproved of one of my routines and she makes her disapproval unmistakable.

I slipped out of the house one night when she was upstairs, and began hammering on the door. She charged downstairs, barking with the high indignation she had evinced one day when she came upon three tree surgeons who seemed to her to be taking down the maple trees in front of the house. With my coat over my head, I charged into the house, roaring like the late Wallace Beery. With a new sound I had never heard before, she turned and seemed to slither upstairs on her stomach, but she stopped at the landing, deciding to hold that defense until it became untenable. I started up the stairs in a Lon Chaney crawl, and halfway up she recognized me. She didn't think it was funny and wouldn't shake hands for several days.

She likes to be taken to a country restaurant a few miles from home, where she is petted and fed, and which she apparently thinks I own, since she challenges people who arrive for dinner after she has got there. She doesn't like big parties, unless they are composed only of the half-dozen persons she truly admires, and she goes out into the kitchen until the last car has driven away. Not long ago, at a house where there were many people, and three or four dogs, she became bored when voices were raised in song, and asked someone to let her out. Half an hour later, the couple that works for us, driving along the road in their car, caught in their headlights a black dog with a yellow collar trotting squarely down the road, and they picked her up. She had come more than a mile from the house of the party she didn't like, and she was on the right road, too, headed for home, but she had a good four miles to go, and that's a long trip for so old a dog. I am confident that she would have got there all right, age or no age.

I said in "Christabel: Part One," something about burying the old poodle under the apple tree. I take it back. I have no doubt now but that she will see me buried first, but she won't lie on my grave for days and nights on end, if I know Christabel. She will be out in the kitchen, stomping her feet, and trying to talk, and asking for the steak platter. What is more, she will get it, too.

THE HOUND

AND

THE GUN

1

2

3

4

5

CHAPTER TWENTY-TWO

The Cockeyed Spaniard

THE ANATOMY OF CONFUSION is a large subject, and I have no intention of writing the standard treatise on it, but I offer to whoever does the most singular of all my cases, the Case of the Cockeyed Spaniard. This remarkable piece of confusion took place in Columbus, Ohio, as long ago as 1922. I lived next door to a young couple named Dan and Janet Henderson at the time. Dan was a well-known reveler of the neighborhood, given to odd companions and peculiar pranks. One afternoon about six o'clock, Janet phoned me and asked me to come over. Her voice sounded wavy and troubled. "What's Dan up to now?" I asked.

She sighed. "He's bringing home a cockeyed Spaniard," she said, "and I simply won't face them both alone."

247

Thurber's Dogs

I slipped my brass knuckles into my pocket and went over to the Henderson house. "The only Spaniards I know of in Columbus," I told Janet, "are a dozen students at Ohio State, but I doubt that they would be cockeyed as early as six o'clock."

It transpired that Dan Henderson had phoned his ominous message while Mrs. Henderson was in the bathtub. Their colored maid Mary had answered the phone. I interviewed Mary in the kitchen. She was popeyed and nervous. The physical stature of the Spaniard and the degree of his intoxication had obviously become magnified in her mind. "I ain't goin' to mess around with no cockeyed Spaniard," she told me flatly. "If he mislests me, I'll hit him with a bottle." While we waited for Dan and his friend to show up, I began to apply my special methods to the case, and before long I had figured it out. No doubt you have, too, since you are probably smarter than I was in 1922.

When Dan came home to his frantic wife, he was carrying the cockeyed Spaniard in his arms, but the fellow was, of course, neither cockeyed nor Spanish. He was sad-eyed, four months old, sleepy, hungry, and definitely sober, as cute a cocker spaniel as you would ever want to see. Mary stubbornly clung to the name she had got over the phone, and her insistence on this pleasant distortion became generally known about town. People would call up the Henderson

248

The Cockeyed Spaniard

house and ask for her and say, "This is the Canine Census Bureau. What kind of dog do you have in your home?"

Mary would always reply promptly and brightly, "He's a cockeyed Spaniard." I often wonder what ever became of her. I hope she is well and happy.

CHAPTER TWENTY-THREE

Lo, Hear the Gentle Bloodhound!

IF BLOODHOUNDS COULD WRITE—all that these wonderful dogs can really do, and it's plenty, is trail lost children and old ladies, and track down lawbreakers and lunatics—they would surely be able to set down more demonstrable truths about themselves than Man has discovered in several centuries of speculation and guesswork, lighted only here and there with genuine research. Books about the St. Bernard, storied angel of the mountain snows, and the German shepherd and other breeds famous for their work as army scouts, city cops, and seeing-eye dogs, sprawl all over the library, but the literature of the English bloodhound, an even greater benefactor of mankind, is meager and sketchy. Only one standard book is available, *Bloodhounds and How to Train Them*, by Dr. Leon F. Whitney of New Haven, first published in 1947 and brought out in a revised edition a few months ago.

Man doesn't even know for sure how the bloodhound got his name. Dr. Whitney, veterinarian, geneticist, and researcher, and many other authorities, subscribe to the respectable theory that the "blood" is short for "blooded," meaning a patrician, an aristocrat, a thoroughbred. My own theory is that the "blood" got into the name because of the ancient English superstitution that giants and other monsters, including the hound with the Gothic head and the miraculously acute nose, could smell the blood of their prey. The giant that roared, "I smell the blood of an Englishman!" had the obscene legendary power, in my opinion, to smell blood through clothing and flesh. Nobody knows to this day the source, nature, or chemistry of the aura that sets off each human being from all others in the sensitive nostrils of every type of scent-hound, but we will get around to that profound mystery further along on this trail. It seems to me, however, that legend and lore are more likely than early breeders and fanciers to have given

Lo, Hear the Gentle Bloodhound!

the bloodhound his name. In any case, it has always had a fearsome sound to the ignorant ear, and one of the gentlest of all species, probably, indeed, the gentlest, has been more maligned through the centuries than any other great Englishman with the exception of King Richard the Third.

Dictionaries, encyclopedias, and other imposing reference volumes approach the bloodhound with an air of gingerly insecurity. Webster's International, touching lightly on the subject, observes, truly enough, that the bloodhound was originally used for hunting game, and adds "especially wounded game." This phrase may have grown out of the imperishable legend of blood scent, but it is also based on the fact that bloodhounds were ever slow and ponderous pursuers, more apt to catch up with a wounded stag or a stricken hart than one of unimpaired fleetness. The staid Encyclopedia Britannica gives our hero scant attention and alludes vaguely to an Italian type of the third century, a scent-hound, without doubt, but not a genuine bloodhound. There were scent-hounds, Dr. Whitney's researches prove, as far back as the age of Xenophon in Greece. Incidentally, the dogs that hunt by sight instead of smell, eminently the swift greyhound, originated, according to Webster, as long ago as 1300 B.C.

The sight-hounds have enjoyed, through the ages,

a romantic tradition, for it is this type of canine hunter that has immemorially appeared in fairy tales, leading the mounted king and his three sons in swift pursuit of the fleet deer which turns out in the end to be an enchanted princess. But the scent-hounds of fiction have usually been terrifying creatures, and they have done their share in bringing libel to the fair name of the bloodhound. The terrible phosphorescent Hound of the Baskervilles, which terrorized the moors and bedeviled Sherlock Holmes and Dr. Watson, was a purebred Conan Doyle hound, but if you ask the average person to identify it, he will almost always say that it was a bloodhound, as savage as all the rest of the breed. Let us sniff a little further along the trail of reference volumes, before setting out on the ancient spoor of the bloodhound itself. The austere Oxford English Dictionary doesn't even attempt to account for the bloodhound's name, but with its famous bloodhound ability to track down sources, comes up with these variants of the name, used in England from 1350 through the eighteenth century: "blod-hounde, bloode hownde, blude hunde, blood hunde, bloud-hound, blod-honde." The name was spelled the way it is today by Oliver Goldsmith, Sir Walter Scott, John Keats ("The wakeful bloodhound rose, and shook his hide"), and Lord Byron, who once wrote "To have set the bloodhound mob on their patrician prey." Here the great hunter is no longer a patrician himself, but he hunts only patricians, as the Belvidere foxhounds, drawn years ago by D. T. Carlisle for *The Sportsman*, hunted only silver fox. The O. E. D., by the way, adds "stolen cattle" to the bloodhound's ancient quarry of wounded stags, wanted criminals, and wandering children. It could have brought the record up to date by putting lost dogs in the list, and at least one cat, which disappeared in an Eastern town not long ago and was found by a bloodhound that had sniffed its sandbox and followed the feline trail faithfully but with ponderous embarrassment, I feel sure.

The first scent-hound, or expert private nose, that stands out clearly in the tapestry of time is the St. Hubert of France, in the eighth century. Some of these castle-and-monastery hounds, after 1066, were imported into England, and from them sprang three English types, the talbot, the staghound, and the bloodhound. Of these, only the bloodhound remains extant. The infamous libel that clings to his name, the legend that he is a dog of awful ferocity began, in this country, before the Civil War, when foxhounds and mongrels were used to hunt down escaped slaves and were trained to fierceness. There may have been a few purebred English bloodhounds in Virginia and other southern states a hundred years ago, but the dogs that pursued Eliza across the ice in *Uncle Tom's Cabin* were crossbred, bar-sinister hounds. It was such beasts that tracked down members of James Andrew's Northern Raiders after they had stolen the famous Iron Horse locomotive at Big Shanty, Georgia, and finally took to the woods of the Southern Confederacy. These inferior pursuers could be bought for five dollars a pair, but the purebred bloodhound then cost fifty dollars a pair. The reputation of the mongrels for ferocity was calculated to deter slaves from making a break for freedom, for if they did and were caught by the dogs, they were sometimes mangled or killed. The trail of a fugitive slave was usually fresh, and any nose-hound could follow it easily. This is also true of the trails of prisoners who escape from prison farms and penitentiaries today, and therefore the so-called "penitentiary hounds" do not need the educated nostrils of a thoroughbred. They are also trained to fierceness, since they must often deal with dangerous criminals.

However the "blood" may have got into our hero's name, it has helped to stain him almost indelibly as a cruel and feral monster. The miraculous finder of lost boys and girls, the brilliant fingerman of thousands of sheriffs' posses, policemen, and private trailers, could be safely trusted not to harm a babe in arms. Dr. Whitney's bloodhounds once found a three-year-

Lo, Hear the Gentle Bloodhound!

old Connecticut girl who had wandered away from her grandmother in a deep bramble of blackberry bushes. The dogs insisted on searching an almost impenetrable swampy region, but were deterred for hours by *Homo sapiens,* in uniform and out, who was positive the child could not have gone that far. When the human beings finally gave the dogs their own way, they dashed into the thicket. Half an hour later the hunting men came upon the little girl, sitting in a pool of water—she had taken off her playsuit to go for a swim. She was naked as a jay bird, but happy as a lark because of the two lovely wrinkled canine playmates she had just "found." Without the help of the hounds, she could never have been traced.

The Oxford Dictionary, with its characteristic erudition, reports that the bloodhound's Latin name is *canis sanguinarius,* a name the Romans never used. Now *sanguinarius* does not mean blooded, in the sense of purebred; it means of or pertaining to blood, and, figuratively, bloody, bloodthirsty, sanguinary. The gentle, good-tempered, well-balanced bloodhound is actually about as fierce as Little Eva, and you simply cannot discover one provable instance of a bloodhound's attacking a child or an adult, including a cornered criminal. Dr. Whitney says the hounds don't even seem to know that teeth were made for biting. It is true that one bloodhound I heard about became

Thurber's Dogs

understandably vexed when his master pulled him off a hot trail, and showed his indignation by a thunderous growl. It is unwise to frustrate a bloodhound who has not come to the end of a trail he is following, and how could this one have known that the bandit he was after had been apprehended, according to a telephone call, fifteen miles ahead?

It has been nearly twenty years since I came upon a flagrant piece of calumny about my friend the bloodhound, in a four-volume set of books called *The Outline of Science, a Plain Story Simply Told,* but my indignation is still as strong as it was then. The anonymous "expert" assigned to write about canines in these books had this to say: "There are few dogs which do not inspire affection; many crave it. But there are some which seem to repel us, like the bloodhound. True, Man has made him what he is. Terrible to look at and terrible to encounter, Man has raised him up to hunt down his fellowman." Accompanying the article was a picture of a dignified and melancholy English bloodhound, about as terrible to look at as Abraham Lincoln, about as terrible to encounter as Jimmy Durante. It pleases me no end that this passage, in its careless use of English, accidentally indicts the human being: "Terrible to look at and terrible to encounter, Man. . . ." Even my beloved, though occasionally cockeyed, Lydekker's *New Nat-*

Lo, Hear the Gentle Bloodhound!

ural History, whose grizzly-bear expert pooh-poohs the idea that grizzly bears are dangerous (it seems they got the reputation of aggressiveness by rolling downhill toward the hunter after they were shot dead), knows better than to accuse the bloodhound of viciousness, or, at any rate, has the good sense to avoid the subject of his nature. Lydekker's bloodhound man contents himself with a detailed and fascinating physical description of the breed, which goes like this. "The most striking and characteristic feature of the bloodhound is its magnificent head, which is considerably larger and heavier in the male than in the female. While generally extremely massive, the head is remarkable for its narrowness between the ears, where it rises into a domelike prominence, terminating in a marked protuberance in the occipital region. The skin of the forehead, like that round the eyes, is thrown into a series of transverse puckers." The Lydekker dog man alludes, in conclusion, to what he calls "a foreign strain of the bloodhound, which is lower on its legs than the English breed."

This foreigner could not possibly be the hound I have been putting into drawings for twenty-five years, because I was only six when the first American edition of Lydekker's *History* was brought out. My dog *is* lower on its legs than a standard bloodhound, although I would scarcely put it that way myself. He got his short legs by accident. I drew him for the first time on the cramped pages of a small memo pad in order to plague a busy realtor friend of mine given to writing down names and numbers while you were trying to talk to him in his office. The hound I draw has a fairly accurate pendulous ear, but his dot of an eye is vastly oversimplified, he doesn't have enough transverse puckers, and he is all wrong in the occipital region. He may not be as keen as a genuine bloodhound, but his heart is just as gentle; he does not want to hurt anybody or anything; and he loves serenity and heavy dinners, and wishes they would go on forever, like the brook.

The late Hendrik Van Loon is the only man I have known well who owned a bloodhound, but he took his back to the kennel where he had bought it, after trying in vain to teach it something besides the fine art of pursuit. Whenever Mr. Van Loon called the dog, he once told me sorrowfully, it took its own good time finding him, although he might be no more than fifty feet away. This bloodhound never went directly to his master, but conscientiously followed his rambling trail. "He was not interested in me or where I was," said Mr. Van Loon. "All he cared about was how I had got there." Mr. Van Loon had made the mistake of assuming that a true bloodhound would fit as cozily into a real living room as my hound does

Lo, Hear the Gentle Bloodhound!

in the drawings. It is a mistake to be sedulously avoided. "I would rather housebreak a moose," the great man told me with a sigh.

The English bloodhound has never been one of the most popular housedogs in the world, but this is not owing solely to the dark slander that has blackened his reputation. He is a large, enormously evident creature, likely to make a housewife fear for her antiques and draperies, and he is not given to frolic and parlor games. He is used to the outdoors. If you want a dog to chase a stick or a ball, or jump through a hoop, don't look at him. "Bloodhounds ain't any good unless you're lost," one little boy told me scornfully. It must be admitted that the cumbersome, jowly tracer of lost persons is somewhat blobbered and slubby (you have to make up words for unique creatures like the bloodhound and the bandersnatch). Compared to breeds whose members are numbered in multiple thousands, the bloodhound is a rare variety, and there may not be more than 1,500 or 2,000 of them in America. An accurate census is discouraged by some bloodhound kennels, many of which are not listed in the *American Kennel Gazette* for their own protection. Some years ago a Connecticut pack of twenty was poisoned, presumably by a friend or relative of some lawbreaker that one or two of the hounds had tracked down. The hounds are bred for two main purposes: to be exhibited at dog shows around the country, and to be trained for police work or private investigation. In 1954, at the annual Eastern Dog Club Show in Boston, a five-year-old bloodhound named Fancy Bombardier was selected as the best dog of all the breeds assembled there, for the first time in the forty-one-year history of the show. This was a rare distinction for our friend, for it was one of the infrequent times a bloodhound in this country ever went Best of Show. Not many judges are as familiar with the show points of a bloodhound as they are with the simpler ones of other breeds. The wondrous Englishman, with his voluminous excess wrinkled flesh, his cathedral head and hooded, pink-hawed eyes, deep-set in their sockets, might seem to some judges too grotesque for prizes, but these are his marks of merit and aristocracy.

Bloodhound-owners themselves disagree about bloodhound types and their comparative appeal, the orthodox school vehemently contending that the purebred hound is the favorite of dog-show galleries, the other school contending that the old patricians repel visitors and are frequently regarded as "hideous." There may yet be a well-defined feud between the two schools. Dr. Whitney, geneticist, eugenicist, and mammalogist, among other things, is one of those who approve of the so-called American-type blood-

Lo, Hear the Gentle Bloodhound!

hound, whose anatomy is less exaggerated. Its "streamlined" conformation is said to be a virtue in trailing, if not an advantage in the show ring. Some authorities believe that this American hound, if judiciously crossbred with the English type, would add a morganatic strain of sturdiness to the Grand Duke's descendants. The English dog, after centuries of pure breeding, does not have a powerful constitution and is subject to certain virus infections and a destructive stomach ailment called "bloat." (Six fine American-owned bloodhounds died of it last year.)

Many state police barracks, but far from enough, have at least one pair of trained bloodhounds. Perhaps the foremost police trainer and trailer in the East is Sergeant W. W. Horton of the state barracks at Hawthorne, New York. He began years ago as a corporal, and for nearly two decades he and his dogs have built up a great record tracking down the crooked and the vanished. They have worked in half a dozen different states, and three years ago Sergeant Horton and his partner were asked by the government of Bermuda to bring their dogs down there to hunt a criminal, notorious for his escapes from prison and his skill in hiding out. They were the first bloodhounds that most Bermudians had seen, and they were not warmly welcomed by the population because of the ancient superstitions about them. The dogs found the coral terrain of Bermuda a good scent-holder, but they were disturbed by crowds of people that followed them, like a gallery at a golf tournament. They traced their man, finally, down to the water's edge, where he had apparently escaped from the island by ship. Sergeant Horton and his partner wore holstered .38 police pistols which astonished the Bermudians, who may keep guns in their homes, but wouldn't dream of displaying one in public. "They thought we were making a movie," Sergeant Horton told me the other day. "Everybody kept looking for the cameras." (I tracked the Sergeant down easily. He was handling the switchboard when I phoned.) Rusty, one of the two Hawthorne hounds that flew to Bermuda, died last winter at the unusual age of fifteen years.

The success of the dogs as trailers depends a great deal on what might be called the dogmanship of their trainers and handlers. Dr. Whitney, who has worked his own hounds with, and sometimes parallel to, the police of Connecticut, New York, and Rhode Island, has often found his man on cases in which official police dogs had failed. Expertness with a canine trailer is a knack, like a green thumb in the garden or a light hand in the kitchen, and some cops never get the hang of it. The training of a bloodhound may begin when the dog is a puppy, capable of toddling a trail only a

Lo, Hear the Gentle Bloodhound!

few yards long, but a two-year-old beginner can sometimes be taught most of the tricks in six weeks; with others it may take six months. They may begin by watching a "runner" disappear from an automobile in which he has left his coat behind. The dog sniffs it carefully and sets out on the trail when the runner is lost to view. Youngsters are often used as runners, and they leave a blazed trail so that the handler can tell if the dogs get off the track. The handicap of time is slowly increased, and so is the number of runners. Eventually, five or more of them set out in single file and it is up to the bloodhound to follow the track of only one when the group scatters, the runner whose coat or cap or shoe the dog has examined with the sharpest nose in the world. He must learn to go up to a youngster whose shoe he has sniffed, paying no attention to another youngster, nearer at hand, who may be holding a piece of liver and smelling to high heaven of reward.

Bloodhounds have done more for humanity than all other canines and most men. Examples of their unique achievements would easily fill two sizable volumes, and I can only select a few at random. Let us begin with the late Madge, a bitch owned many years ago by Dr. C. Fosgate of Oxford, New York. Madge was once called upon to trace a lost boy in a town upstate. The trail was twenty-four hours old. Madge climbed fences, wandered through yards, went down alleys, and presently asked to be let into a grocery. Inside, she trotted to a crate of oranges, then crossed over and placed both front paws on the counter. The grocer then remembered that a little boy had come in the morning before, taken an orange from the crate, and paid for it at the counter. The end of the trail was tragic: Madge came to a pier end at a river and plunged unhesitatingly into the water. The boy had been drowned there.

For more than a quarter of a century, up to October 1954, to be exact, the record for following the coldest trail, 105 hours old, was held by a male named Nick Carter, generally considered to have been the greatest bloodhound that ever lived. He was part of the most fabulous pack of bloodhounds in our history, one belonging to the late Captain Volney G. Mullikin of Kentucky. An entire volume could be devoted to the Mullikin hounds alone, and to their colorful master. From about 1897 until 1932, the Mullikin hounds brought about the capture of 2,500 criminals and wrongdoers in Kentucky, Tennessee, West Virginia, and other states. A hundred of them were wanted for murder, others for rape, or burglary, or moonshining, or sabotage (Captain Mullikin got $5,000 from a West Virginia coal company for tracking down a gang of saboteurs), and almost every other crime in

Lo, Hear the Gentle Bloodhound!

the calendar, including arson. Nick Carter's old cold trail of four days and nine hours brought to justice a man who had burned down a hen house, but he closed a total of six hundred cases, most of them major, during his great career, and no other dog has ever come close to that accomplishment. The Nick Carter case that I have encountered most often in my researches was one in which he brought to justice a group of mischievous youngsters who, for many weeks, had been in the habit of throwing rocks through the windows of houses at night and easily avoiding capture by the police. Nick was finally allowed to sniff one of the rocks which had been pulled out from under a bed with a cane and placed on a newspaper. Nick got the first of the young miscreants in a matter of hours, and the other boys were soon rounded up.

Captain Mullikin, whose photograph shows a lean, rangy, keen-eyed man, was brave to the point of foolhardiness, and more than once stood off lynching mobs, protecting a prisoner whose guilt had not been proved. He and his dogs were in the bloody midst of the Howard-Baker and Hatfield-McCoy mountain feuds, and ran to earth a number of assassins on both sides of each of these family wars. The captain's body showed scores of buckshot scars, most of them on his legs. The fame of the Kentucky pack and its valiant leader spread as far as Cuba, and the government of

that island hired the Kentuckians, on a six-months'
contract, to capture a notorious bandit. The hounds
caught up with the man in a matter of days, but the
Cuban government insisted on paying the full six-
months' fee agreed upon.

When Captain Mullikin died, he left much of his
bloodhoundiana, including a mountain of newspaper
clippings reciting the glorious feats of the captain
and his dogs, to Dr. Whitney, to whose book I am in-
debted for these all too brief Mullikin facts. The doctor was also given the harness that had been worn by
Nick Carter on his hundreds of cases. When a hound
starts out on a trail, his leash is unfastened from his
collar and snapped onto his harness, and this forms
the go-ahead signal, along with some such invariable
command as "Find him" or "Go get 'em." Incidentally, there are two kinds of working bloodhounds, known as open trailers—the ones that bay
as they go—and mute trailers—the dogs that give no
sign of their approach—and you can get into a rousing
argument about comparative values in this field, too.
Hounds of any kind hunting by themselves, alone or
in pairs or packs, always bay on the trail of an animal
quarry, but the leashed bloodhound can be taught
either sound or silence in trailing a human being. No
bloodhound ever gives tongue when he gets off the
scent, which, it should be pointed out, is by no means

the mere width of a footprint, but can sometimes be picked up by the dogs over an area of a hundred feet or more.

I called one day on the eight bloodhounds owned by Thomas Sheahan, a factory worker and past president of the American Bloodhound Club, which has only seventy members and is now headed by Mrs. Clendenin J. Ryan. One of hers, Champion Rye of Panther Ledge, beat out Mr. Sheahan's Fancy Bombardier for best of breed at a show last April. Fancy and Rye had met a number of times, however, and the former holds the edge in victories. The Sheahan hounds are neighbors of mine, kenneled at Torrington, twenty miles away. The chief of the pack is, of course, Fancy Bombardier, a couchant hound in the best tradition of austere and pensive Rodinesque posture. A grown poodle poses with the professional grace of an actress, but a bloodhound resembles a Supreme Court Justice gravely submitting to the indignity of being photographed. Bloodhounds may look exactly alike to the layman, but they are not turned out of a rigid mold, like cast-iron lawn dogs. Bombardier's son, Essex Tommy, whose late grandfather had a fine trailing record with the Bethany State Police Barracks in Connecticut, is a wag, a gayheart, with the bloodhound habit of rearing up and planting his big friendly paws on your chest. This affable bloodhound mannerism has been known to frighten a cornered culprit, who does not realize his big pursuer merely wants to shake hands, like the American colonel that captured Hermann Goering at the end of the war.

The Sheahan hounds are bred for show, not trailing, although a few have joined the Connecticut State Police. One of the hounds kept digging solemnly deep into the ground while I was there, hunting for the roots of a tree, which all dogs love to chew. A nine-months-old female got into a loud altercation with a fourteen-year-old German shepherd—something about a missing bone—but there was no biting, only argument and accusation. As puppies, bloodhounds are almost as playful as other dogs, but they soon become sedentary and are interested in no game except professional hide-and-seek. They are brought up outdoors, to thicken their coats and toughen them, but they have to be introduced to rough weather gradually. Once acclimatized, a sound dog may be able to sleep in the snow without chill or frostbite. They are neither climbers nor jumpers, and often have to be lifted over fences and other obstacles. Worn out after a long trail, they may have to be carried and fall asleep easily in their trainers' arms. Mr. Sheahan pulled down the lower eyelid of one patient bloodhound, to show its deep-set reddish eye, which seems to be slowly on its way to becoming vestigial. The stronger the nose, the weaker the eye, generally speaking, and bloodhounds sometimes bump into things on a trail. "You shouldn't be able to see a bloodhound's eye at a distance of thirty feet," Mr. Sheahan said. This is a show point in a true bloodhound's favor. Bloodhounds have a short vocabulary, and few changes of inflection or intonation. Fancy Bombardier kept saying "Who?" deepening the volume as his questioning went on. "*Who?*" he demanded. "Ralph!" I barked. "*Who?*" he roared. "Ralph, Ralph Rolf," I said, and so the stolid cross-examination continued.

The bloodhound is not a commercial dog, and few kennel owners break even financially. A good male puppy usually brings about a hundred dollars, rarely more than three hundred, and eight hundred to a thousand dollars is a high price nowadays for a trained adult of either sex. The first bloodhounds brought into this country from England in this century, around 1905, included some that had cost from $2,000 to $3,500. The prices got lower as the popularity of the breed slowly began to decline. It has come up sharply in recent years, but even so, only 195 new bloodhounds were registered with the American Kennel Club last year. Thomas Sheahan and another eminent bloodhound man, Clarence Fischer of Kings-

Thurber's Dogs

ton, New York, recently recommended a $550 perfect male specimen to George Brooks of LaCrosse, Wisconsin, who bought the dog on their say-so without having seen it. Mr. Fischer, whom some of his colleagues call the most dedicated bloodhound man in America, if not the world, owns the finest and most extensive collection of bloodhoundiana in the country, and has known personally most of the leading American owners and trainers. George Brooks, who works in a drugstore when he is not on the trail, is considered one of the outstanding tracers. His dogs often work at night, since they are less distracted by sights and sounds, and young dogs just learning the trade do much better in the dark. The Brooks hounds specialize in city trailing, and their services are often required by police departments in the Middle West, but they can take on a country job and do just as well. Last winter they followed the tragic trail of two little boys to a hole in the ice of a river where they had drowned.

Most of the trails of lost children and adults fortunately end in the discovery of the persons alive and well. Some police authorities approve of perpetuating the libel that a bloodhound is a savage beast, accustomed to tearing his quarry to bits when he comes upon it. The purpose of this wrong-minded philosophy is to deter evil-doers, and make them

Lo, Hear the Gentle Bloodhound!

think twice before committing a crime and seeking to escape. It is a badly thought-out reversion to the theory and practice of southern slaveowners a hundred years ago and, the point of morality aside, it is calculated to cause the parents of wandering children to fear the use of bloodhounds.

There is a widespread belief, among the uninitiated, that the bloodhound's usefulness in tracking down criminals came to an end with the era of the automobile and the advent of the getaway car. This is only partly true. It is common knowledge that our olfactory genius is interested in automobiles only for what they may contain in the way of human odors, and could not possibly tell a Buick from a Packard, or one tire from another. Everybody also knows that no hound, even if it were able to follow a tire trail, could trace an automobile over hundreds or thousands of miles. But these self-evident facts by no means completely hamstring or footcuff the relentless pursuers. Many fleeing criminals abandon their cars sooner or later, usually alongside a wooded area, thus becoming a setup for bloodhounds. The dogs will get into an abandoned car, inhale a long snoutful of evidence, and set out gleefully and confidently on the track into the woods. They can tell more about the driver or other occupants of an empty motorcar than the police experts in any laboratory. And, remarkable to say, bloodhounds have been known to follow the hot, short trail of a car by picking up, some yards off the road, the scent of the fugitive, if they have previously been able to sniff some personal belonging of his. One hound trotted in a ditch, parallel to the highway, for four miles, apparently detecting with ease the scent of his quarry, car or no car. This particular fugitive had made the mistake of turning into a driveway, four miles from his point of departure, and there was the car, and there was the man, and there, finally, was the hound, ready to shake hands and be congratulated.

This is probably the point at which I should dwell, briefly and in all bewilderment, upon just what it is that human scent consists of. All anybody seems to know is that the distinctive human smell the bloodhound selects from all others must have the infinite variability of fingerprints. Only the bloodhound comprehends this scent, which is so sharp to him and so mysterious to us, and all he has ever said about it is "Who?" Some bloodhound men think of the scent as a kind of effluvium, an invisible exudation that clings low to the earth, about the footprints of men. Whatever it may be, a few facts are definitely known about certain of its manifestations. Dampness, especially that of light rain or dew, often serves to bring out the scent, and it is further preserved by "cover,"

Lo, Hear the Gentle Bloodhound!

which, in the argot of the trailer, means underbrush, thicket, low-spreading plants and bushes, and the like. Bloodhounds are frequently handicapped by what is technically known as the "fouling" of a trail by sightseers and other careless humans. Wind also adds to the troubles of a hound, along with thoughtless trampling by men, in the case of a hunt over snow. One of the hounds belonging to Mr. and Mrs. Robert Noerr of Stamford, Connecticut, is now working out of Anchorage, Alaska, helping to find persons lost in the snows.

The 105-hour record for cold trailing, so long held by the celebrated Nick Carter, was shattered in October 1954 by the well-nigh incredible achievement of three bloodhounds belonging to Norman W. Wilson of Los Gatos, California, a former navy pilot who dedicated himself to the training of bloodhounds after a friend of his had become lost in the Everglades and was found by some Florida hounds. On October 9, 1954, a man and his wife and their thirteen-year-old son went deer hunting in a heavily wooded region of Oregon, thick with second-growth fir and a dense undergrowth of ferns and brush. Just a week later their car was found parked near the woods. The sheriff of the county, aided by two hundred men, an airplane and a helicopter, searched the almost impenetrable area without avail for six days. Wilson and his dogs arrived by plane, and the dogs picked up the ancient scent near the car, using as a scent guide a pair of the wife's stockings. Their leashes were fastened to their harness and the command "Find them!" was given at 9:45 on the night of October 22, 322 hours after the family was thought to have left their car. The dogs "cast" in wide circles, trying to pick up the trail, until three o'clock the next morning, and resumed the search shortly after six o'clock. There had been rains on the night of October 10 and later, and the underbrush and ferns were wet. Fifteen hours after they had taken up the search, or 337 hours after the supposed entrance of the family into the woods, one of the hounds led its trailer to the body of the youngster. The parents were subsequently found, also dead. Mr. Wilson and the sheriff and other officials later submitted the story of the remarkable search, in affidavit form, to the Bloodhound Club, and it seems likely that the amazing new record will be officially accepted. The hounds had led the human searchers in a different direction from that which the sheriff and his two hundred men had taken, in their own dogless and fruitless search. Mr. Wilson, it should be said, receives no reward for his services and those of his hounds, beyond the expenses involved in a hunt. He had offered to help after reading about the missing persons in the newspapers. Nobody had thought to send for bloodhounds.

Lo, Hear the Gentle Bloodhound!

Curiously enough, no bloodhound man seems ever to have experimented to find out how many hours, or days, or perhaps even months or years, the scent of a man or a woman or a child might still cling to something that had once been worn. It is an obvious and interesting area of research, and I am sure the dogs would love it.

One of my favorite bloodhounds is Symbol of Kenwood, a two-year-old from one of the excellent kennels on the West Coast, and a member of the New Mexico Mounted Patrol. Last December Symbol traced two men, wanted for the murder of an Albuquerque policeman, down to the edge of the Rio Grande, promptly hit the water and swam across the river and pointed out his men. They had thought the broad expanse of water would frustrate any pursuing bloodhound. Symbol's feat made up for his impish delinquency of a few days earlier, when he had dug his way out of his kennel and wandered off. He was gone for forty-eight hours, and members of the Mounted Patrol looked for him in vain. He came home, finally, in excellent spirits, having presumably backtracked his own trail. He must have had a twinkle in his grave deep-set eyes as he rejoined the tired and baffled patrol, and I hope he wasn't punished too much. Everybody probably had his own theory as to where Symbol had gone, and everybody was wrong, as Man so often is in dealing with the bloodhound breed. These patient dogs have used, many a time and oft, their one monosyllabic interrogation in dialogue with men, who think their own wisdom is so superior. I wish I could be present some day to hear one of these man-and-dog conversations. Let us say that a parent, or a police officer, or a posse man is speaking first, like this:

"No child could possibly have got through that hedge, according to Sheriff Spencer and Police Chief MacGowan."

"Who?"

And here, gentle reader, let us leave our amazing hero, with the last, and only truly authoritative word.

A Glimpse of the Flatpaws

I F THE PATIENT and devoted English bloodhound
is a plainclothesman, the German shepherd is a
harness bull. Until six years ago, eight or more German shepherds trotted beats, each accompanied by a
police officer, over in Brooklyn. The canine cops had
all been presented to the Brooklyn Police Department by private citizens, but they gradually died off,
or were retired, and finally no new ones appeared to
take their place. They were highly proficient, perfectly trained dog cops, and they brought many a
felon to justice. This squad of Brooklyn flatpaws
contained one policewoman named Peggy, whose record was just as good as that of the males. I went over
to Brooklyn years ago for *The New Yorker's* "Talk
of the Town" and met one of the police dogs, Nero,
who was four years old at the time. We didn't shake

hands. He growled low when I took a step toward
him. "These dogs don't regard any man as their
friend," Nero's partner, Patrolman Michael Mulcare, told me. I went back and sat down, and Nero
stopped growling, but he kept his eye on me. An
active, handsome, glossy animal, he wore his full
equipment: collar, leash, and large leather muzzle
with a broad, hard end. "They knock guys down with
that muzzle," said Mulcare, "if they try to get away."

Nero walked over and sniffed me. "Hello, doggie,"
I said politely. Nero growled again.

"Don't move," said Mulcare. I didn't move. Mulcare commanded the dog to lie down, and he did.
Then he was led away. "You can move now," said
his partner.

Each dog patrolled a night beat in Flatbush with
his officer. The patrolmen stayed on the streets, but,
at the command "Search," the dogs went down dark
alleys, into areaways, and over fences into the lawns
of private houses, sniffing around for intruders. If a
dog found a man—whether burglar, householder,
swain throwing pebbles at a nursemaid's window, or
whomever—he stood bristling beside him, growling
loudly and ominously till the patrolman came up.
The dog never attacked unless the man ran—or
pulled a gun. If he ran, the dog dashed between his
legs and tripped him, or made a flying tackle at the
small of his back and knocked him down. If he pulled

a gun, the dog attacked even more viciously, knocking the man down, working up to his gun hand, and, with claws and muzzle, disarming him. Gunfire merely infuriated a trained German shepherd.

The dogs practiced each day, going up ladders, climbing walls, getting into windows. Now and then at Police Department graduations—and at the Westminster Show—they put on exhibitions. They had been awarded many prizes, which were kept at the Police Academy. Once a shepherd named Rex, investigating a house closed for the season, grew suspicious of an open window on the back porch and went in to look around. When his growls and snarls brought his human partner, Rex had cornered in an upstairs room two thieves who were only too glad to surrender to a less dangerous cop.

If Brooklyn had maintained its night patrol of police dogs, they could have broken up the gang of youthful murderers that recently infested its parks and shocked the world with their meaningless killings. But the German shepherds in America have gradually been retired from police duty since the war, and are now known mainly for their work as Seeing Eye dogs. England has got far ahead of us in the use of trained shepherds to keep down nocturnal crime in the parks of its large cities. Scotland Yard has a force of more than one hundred and fifty Alsatians, and as a result of this alert patrol there were only thirteen

Thurber's Dogs

cases of purse snatching in London's Hyde Park in 1954. In 1946, when the night watch was begun, there were eight hundred and thirty cases of purse snatching in that park.

I saw the Scotland Yard dogs in training when I was in London last June. I called at the Yard one morning and was taken out to the headquarters of the dogs in a police Humber, accompanied by Chief Superintendent John Tickle, then in charge of the flatpaws, and Chief Inspector Morgan Davies, who was about to take his turn in supervising the activities of the Alsatians. These dogs are actually German shepherds under an alias. The breed developed a reputation for ferocity in Germany even before the First World War, and the name was changed in England to free the dog from its stigma of savagery. The police dogs of Germany were trained by the use of whips and spiked collars, which tended to make them hostile to all men. The London dogs, as well as those used in Liverpool, Manchester and Birmingham, undergo a fourteen-weeks course of training during which only kindness and patience are practiced by the dogs' handlers.

Unlike the shepherds of Germany and of Brooklyn, the Alsatians wear no muzzles and they are brought up in the homes of their handlers, usually married men with children. This has made them, if not exactly affable, far less fierce than the dogs of Germany, and considerably more hospitable than the old Brooklyn squad. I found that I could move among the Alsatians without being threatened or even insulted. The thirty young dogs I watched going through their first two weeks of routine lessons kept up a constant clamor, each in its own individual tone of voice, but there was no deep growling. One dog addressed me in a low singsong, something between a bartender's snarl and the crooning of a baby. I think he was daring me to cut and run.

I was shown how the dogs go about finding a man hidden in a tree, climbing ladders and fences, and chasing and pulling to earth an "escaping criminal." Each of the dogs took its turn chasing the man who posed as the fugitive and dragging him to the ground by seizing his sleeve just above the wrist. During each of these acts, the other dogs kept up a continual whining, tugging at their leashes and begging for the signal "Get him!" This is the part of their work they like best, and they have brought down many a culprit who has tried to break away from the handlers.

The dogs have an excellent record for good behavior, on and off duty. Their work has become known far and wide; last year two London-trained Alsatians were added to the police force of Bermuda, and while I was at the training grounds, twenty miles from London, two officers from Lebanon were being schooled in the handling of shepherds. Superintendent Tickle told me, above the babel of the rookies, that the Alsatians were presented to Scotland Yard by private owners. Thirty per cent of the canine candidates for the police force turn out to be unequipped for the work, because of too much pugnacity, or too much gentleness, or a downright lack of interest in climbing things or chasing people. These dogs are returned to their former masters as a rule, but some of the more aggressive ones join the Army or the Air Corps, where they are used as watch dogs for military establishments and air fields. Such installations are secure against saboteurs or night prowlers of any kind when they are guarded by a trained German shepherd.

Labradors, which were originally used, gradually disappeared from the police department because of a curious and false belief that this breed is not aggressive enough to deter criminals. The very existence of the Alsatian patrol, on the other hand, because of the German shepherd's indelible reputation, acts as a preventive of crime in the parks of London, as it would in those of Brooklyn and other parts of New York City. Knowing this from his years of experience with the dogs, Superintendent Tickle wrote a letter to the Police Commissioner of New York, explaining the work of his Alsatians, but he had not received a reply after more than six months. Police officers from Germany, as well as almost every other European country, have travelled to Wickham in Kent, where the

A Glimpse of the Flatpaws

dogs are trained, to act as observers of this most famous of police-dog patrols, but New York has not yet sent any officer to Scotland Yard.

The training of a German shepherd requires as much dogmanship in its handler as the training of a bloodhound, and not every officer is fitted for the job. It may be, for all I know, that Brooklyn's postwar patrolmen turned out to lack the special knack required for working with a dog as a partner. The Brooklyn system of training was a modification of the German system, without its whips and spiked collars, and what Superintendent Tickle and his successor would like to impress upon modern police departments is the efficacy of educating the dogs in the Scotland Yard manner. The dog that lives in its handler's home is more adaptable to training than the one that sees its partner only when the night beat gets under way.

My day at Wickham began at eleven o'clock in the morning, with tea in Superintendent Tickle's office out there. I signed a handsome guest book, a gift to the Wickham Headquarters from Douglas Fairbanks, who had recently made a film called *Police Dog* with the co-operation of Scotland Yard and its Alsatians. The walls of the office were hung with photographs of some of the outstanding heroes of the dog patrol, including the only dog in the force that was ever shot at. British criminals rarely carry guns. This dog was nicked in the ear by one bullet, and three other shots went wild before he closed in on his assailant and brought him down. Even though the dogs wear no muzzles, they never mangle or maul their quarry, but simply hold him until their human partner arrives to take over. A Labrador called Big Ben, who has been with the patrol since it began, has a place of honor in the photograph gallery, since he has brought about one hundred and thirty-three arrests during his nine-year career. Big Ben has little use for Alsatians, and, to prove that his own breed is as tough as any, if not tougher, he is always willing to take on any two Alsatians at the same time, the best day they ever saw.

Superintendent Tickle (who has recently been promoted and reassigned) is not a bloodhound man, and I was astonished to discover that he regards bloodhounds as lacking in courage. Inspector Davies had nothing to say about this theory, but I expressed my opinion one day in the London *Daily Mail*. I tried to point out that the difference between the German shepherd and the bloodhound is purely one of temperament and aptitude, like the difference between the patrolman and the plainclothes detective. I admitted that the bloodhound cannot climb ladders or fences, that it has never been known to knock anybody down except by accident, and that it would no sooner climb through an open window, looking for intruders, burly or otherwise, than I would, or my poodle Christabel. This is a matter of discretion, not a proof of cowardice, and it has kept me alive for sixty years, Christabel for fifteen, and the bloodhound breed for close to a thousand years.

I have no doubt that Big Ben could outdo a trained bloodhound in every aspect of police work except one, the successful following of an old, cold trail. The nose of the German shepherd, like that of the Labrador, has its limitations, and it must invariably give up on ancient trails that a bloodhound could take in his stride. In 1951, the Bloodhound Association of England challenged the Alsatians to a field trial, and the bloodhounds came out on top, but it was not a conclusive test because a lot of things went wrong, including some of the dogs on both sides, and their handlers. There are only two bloodhound trainers left in England who were training dogs before the war, most of the other trainers having been killed in action or grown too old for this highly specialized work. The little group of devoted private owners and breeders of bloodhounds in England goes doggedly on, however, holding a field trial every year, occasionally lending its hounds to the police of a city or town here and there in the British Isles.

The great English bloodhound, in his native land, has not kept up with his American brother, but he is still on his feet, and still willing and eager to take on police-trained Alsatians over a trail from twenty-four

Thurber's Dogs

hours to two weeks old, or even colder than that. Perhaps some day there may be an annual international field trial in which the best German shepherds and bloodhounds of the United States and Great Britain take part. I shall be glad to present a Thurber Cup to be awarded each year at this competition. And may the best bloodhound win.

THE HOUND

AND

THE BUG

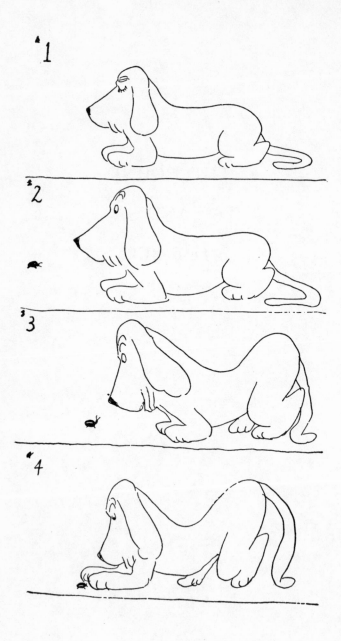

°5

°6

⁷7

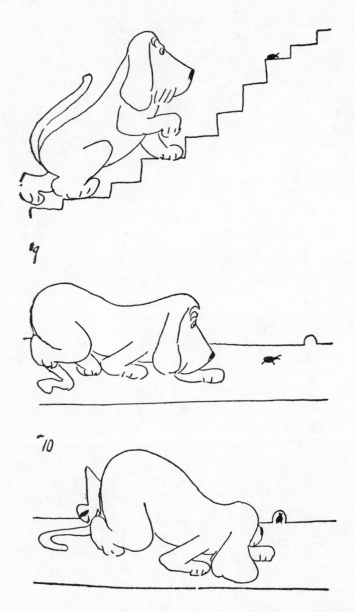

Outstanding Paperback Books